PROPERTY LAW SIMULATIONS

By

John G. Sprankling
Distinguished Professor of Law
University of the Pacific
McGeorge School of Law

BRIDGE TO PRACTICE

WEST®

Mat #41188090

© 2013 LEG, Inc. d/b/a West Academic Publishing

610 Opperman Drive
St. Paul, MN 55123
1-800-313-9378

Printed in the United States of America

West, West Academic Publishing, and West Academic are trademarks of West Publishing Corporation, used under license.

ISBN: 978–0–314–27788–6

DEDICATION

For Gail, Tom, and Doug

ACKNOWLEDGMENTS

I thank my colleague and friend Michael Vitiello for his leadership in developing the Bridge to Practice Series. I also wish to thank Louis Higgins and everyone at West for sharing our vision that experiential learning will be an increasingly important component of American legal education in future years.

In preparing the book, I was benefited by the experience and insights of many other colleagues. Special thanks go to Cary Bricker, Ray Coletta, and John Myers for their valuable comments, to Doug Sprankling for his proofreading, and to Cathleen Mulloy for her computer wizardry. I also thank Dean Jay Mootz and Associate Deans Anne Bloom and Julie Davies for their support. Finally, I thank my former Property students who have helped me to understand the value of experiential learning.

Most importantly, I thank my wife Gail Heckemeyer for her loving encouragement and careful proofreading.

TABLE OF CONTENTS

INTRODUCTION

A. WHY USE SIMULATIONS?

This book contains simulation exercises for use in the standard first-year Property class, as a supplement to your casebook. At this point, you might logically ask why your professor has assigned the book. Here are two answers.

1. DEVELOPING PROFESSIONAL SKILLS

For decades, many have complained that American legal education focuses too much on theory and largely ignores skills. Two studies dominate the scholarship on this topic. The first is a 1992 report by an American Bar Association task force chaired by Robert MacCrate, *Legal Education and Professional Development—An Educational Continuum*. The second is the Carnegie Foundation report *Educating Lawyers: Preparation for the Practice of Law*, published in 2007. Although they differ in methodology and scope, both studies agree on one key point: law schools need to place more emphasis on professional skills.

The MacCrate report had little impact on legal education. But the Carnegie report has been more successful, prompting many law schools to make curricular changes that expand opportunities for experiential learning. The relative success of the Carnegie report stems, in part, from changes in the legal environment. In general, law firms are less willing to devote substantial time to training new associates because of competitive pressures. As a result, there is increased demand for new lawyers who are familiar with professional skills, even if they have not yet mastered them.

These exercises give you the opportunity to begin learning core skills during your first year of law school. They accordingly provide a foundation for more advanced study of these skills during your second and third years.

2. UNDERSTANDING SUBSTANTIVE LAW

Major advances in learning theory have been made in recent years. Empirical research shows that interactive exercises are useful in helping students understand both the nature of substantive doctrines and how they are used in our legal system.

Learning is a process. In general, the quality of learning is enhanced when students are actively involved in using legal concepts, rather than simply reading a text or hearing discussion. For example, a central concept in landlord-tenant law is the implied warranty of habitability: the owner of a residential apartment impliedly promises his tenant that the apartment will be fit for human habitation. If the owner breaches this obligation, the tenant may withhold rent and assert this breach as a defense if the owner tries to evict her. You will understand this doctrine better if you have the opportunity to assert the defense as the tenant's attorney in a simulated eviction trial, rather than merely hearing the doctrine discussed in the classroom.

In short, the exercises in this book will help you learn property law by making it more relevant and more concrete.

B. CONTENTS OF THIS BOOK

1. TWELVE CASE FILES

The book contains twelve exercises, each dealing with a different topic that is commonly taught in the first-year Property class: adverse possession; gifts; estates and future interests; concurrent ownership; marital property; landlord-tenant law; real property sales; nuisance law; easements; covenants, conditions, and restrictions; eminent domain; and takings. Your class may not study all of these topics, because course coverage differs from professor to professor. But the chances are good that your class will cover most of these topics.

Each exercise is based on a case file of realistic documents that concern a property dispute, such as letters, deeds, and pleadings. Each exercise asks you to take on the role of an attorney representing a client in a dispute or, potentially, a judge who is asked to decide the dispute.

All of the exercises are set in the hypothetical state of Madison. Madison is a state that has little law and, accordingly, is heavily influenced by precedents from other jurisdictions.

Notice that the dates in the exercises use a special format which prevents the book from becoming chronologically obsolete. For example, instead of using a date such as October 1, 2013, the text might use October 1, YR-00. YR-00 refers to the current year; YR-01 to the previous year; YR-02 to two years ago; YR-03 to three years ago; and so forth.

2. TWO SKILLS: NEGOTIATION AND ADVOCACY

The exercises are designed to introduce you to two core skills: negotiation and advocacy. But the exercises are flexible enough to be used in different ways if your professor chooses. For example, each advocacy exercise can be utilized as the basis for a negotiation or a writing assignment.

Seven exercises focus on the skill of negotiation. Every lawyer negotiates. You may never try a case or draft a contract, but you will negotiate. Negotiation is a skill that can be learned, practiced, and eventually mastered. Many attorneys have never studied the subject systematically, but instead have picked up their techniques over time by trial and error. The goal of these exercises is to expose you to the fundamental principles which underlie any negotiation, so that you have a structured approach to the subject. Accordingly, each such exercise will introduce you to two basic negotiation tools. You will be expected to use those tools in your negotiation. As you progress through later exercises, your collection of negotiation tools will expand, and you will be expected to use all of them.

Five exercises focus on the skill of advocacy. Even if you do not anticipate doing litigation, it is valuable to understand the litigation process. And if you are interested in litigation, these exercises will give you a brief introduction to the subject. Two of the exercises are short jury trials, in which you may have the opportunity to be both (a) an attorney or witness and (b) a juror. As an attorney, you will have the opportunity to argue your case before a student jury. As a juror, you will evaluate the competing merits of the arguments for each side in reaching a decision. The three remaining exercises are closing arguments to a judge after a court trial. Here your task is to argue your case before a judge, based on the evidence in the case file before you. Depending on how your professor chooses to structure the exercise, you may instead act as a judge.

Good luck!

CHAPTER 1

ADVERSE POSSESSION

A. INTRODUCTION

The exercise in this chapter gives you the opportunity to explore the law of adverse possession, which is a core principle in American property law. The same principle is found in the domestic legal systems of most nations.

This exercise—like many in the book—is designed to introduce you to the skill of negotiation. In a negotiation, each attorney typically seeks to justify her bargaining position by explaining why the law favors her side. In theory, the outcome of a negotiation should reflect the strength of each side's legal position. Thus, knowledge of substantive law is an integral part of any negotiation.

This chapter has three parts. First, it provides you with an overview of the relevant law. Next, it discusses two basic negotiation techniques. Finally, it gives you a negotiation exercise involving adverse possession law, based on a case file of documents. The exercise requires you to participate in negotiating the resolution of an adverse possession dispute.

B. OVERVIEW OF THE LAW

Adverse possession is a controversial doctrine. In a nutshell, if A occupies B's land for a long enough period of time while meeting certain conditions, A obtains title to the land without payment or any need for B's consent. Perhaps you are tempted to ask: Isn't this just theft? The answer, of course, is no. One reason most property casebooks cover adverse possession is because it provides a useful window into the policies that underlie American property law.

Like most property doctrines, adverse possession is a creature of state law, not federal law, and is largely based on case law. Accordingly, the precise requirements and terminology vary somewhat from state to state. In most jurisdictions, however, an occupant acquires title to land by adverse possession if his possession is: actual, exclusive, open and notorious, adverse and hostile, and continuous for the required period. In a minority of states, including California and New York, these traditional case law elements are supplemented by special statutory requirements.

The exercise below is set in the hypothetical state of Madison, which follows the majority approach by requiring the following elements:

1. *Actual possession:* The claimant must use the land in the same manner that a reasonable owner would, given its character, location, and nature. For example, someone seeking to adversely possess farm land must, at a minimum, use the land for farming just as a reasonable owner would do. In many states, the use of land solely for recreational purposes is not considered to be actual possession; this question has never been addressed by Madison courts.

2. *Exclusive possession:* The claimant's possession cannot be shared with the owner or the public in general. In order to interrupt the claimant's exclusive possession, the owner must retake possession by meeting the actual possession requirement above. The owner who merely visits her land has not retaken possession.

3. *Open and notorious possession:* The claimant's possession must be so visible and obvious that if the owner made a reasonable inspection of the land, he would become aware that someone was asserting a claim to title. The purpose of this requirement is to give notice to an inspecting owner.

4. *Adverse and hostile possession:* This is the most difficult element to understand, partly because there is a split of authority and partly because different states use different terminology to describe essentially the same concept. All jurisdictions agree that this requirement is not met if the claimant enters into possession with the consent of the owner. The other part of the requirement involves the claimant's state of mind. Some states mandate that the claimant act in *good faith*: she must actually believe that she is the owner of the land. Historically, a few states insisted that the claimant must act in *bad faith*: she must intend to take the land from the owner, knowing that she does not own it herself. Today the majority view is that the claimant's state of mind is *irrelevant*. Madison law follows the majority approach.

5. *Continuous possession:* The claimant's possession must be as continuous as a reasonable owner's possession would be, given the character, location, and nature of the land. For example, because the reasonable owner of a residential condominium unit would presumably live there on a full-time basis, a claimant would be required to do this as well. In contrast, sporadic uses of wild and unimproved land may be deemed continuous if this is how frequently a reasonable owner would use such land.

6. *Statutory period:* The claimant must satisfy the above elements for a period of time defined by the relevant state statute. Depending on the state, the period may range from 5 years to 40 years. The adverse possession period in Madison is 5 years.

C. NEGOTIATION TECHNIQUES

This section will introduce you to two very basic negotiation tools that you will use in the first exercise. As the Introduction notes, you will be provided with additional tools during later exercises. Accordingly, your collection of negotiation tools will increase as the class proceeds. You will be expected to use all of them in future negotiations.

1. *Develop a plan for the negotiation:* Negotiation requires advance planning. Just as an experienced aircraft pilot plots out a route before takeoff, a good negotiator develops a plan for how the negotiation should proceed. In formulating the plan, a negotiator will want to consider both the goals she seeks to attain and the methods that she will use to reach those goals. Inevitably, a certain amount of improvisation is required in almost any negotiation because the negotiator will confront an adversary with quite a different plan. The best plan is definite, yet flexible.

2. *Set appropriate goals for the negotiation:* Your negotiation will be more successful if your plan includes goals. A goal should be: (a) specific; (b) justifiable; (c) reasonably optimistic; and (d) authorized by the client. A goal must be specific enough to inform the manner in which the attorney conducts the negotiation, because the point of the negotiation is to reach that goal. A goal should be justifiable because this provides legitimacy for the attorney's position. It is also helpful to establish a goal that is reasonably optimistic, while realizing that the client may ultimately be forced to accept something less. Finally, as a matter of legal ethics, the goal of the representation is set by the client, not by the attorney. An attorney may make or accept an offer only if she is specifically authorized to do so by her client.

D. THE JOHNSON-STONE DISPUTE

In this simulation, you will be an attorney involved in a negotiation concerning an adverse possession claim to 20 acres of forest land in Madison. Elmer F. Johnson, the adverse claimant, contends that he acquired title to the land from Laura M. Stone, the record owner. You will represent either Johnson or Stone.

A person who satisfies all the requirements for adverse possession automatically acquires title to the land involved as a matter of law. Yet the public land records will not reflect such a transfer of title unless the successful adverse possessor takes affirmative action, either by recording a judgment confirming her ownership following a quiet title action or by recording a deed from the former record owner. Where an adverse possessor has clearly acquired title, it makes sense for the former owner to cooperate in resolving any title dispute by providing a deed to the new owner. This avoids litigation, minimizing costs and inconvenience for both parties. Of course, where there is an actual dispute about whether the adverse possession requirements have been satisfied, the record owner will refuse such a request, setting the stage for either negotiation or litigation. As you will see in the case file below, Stone rejects Johnson's claim that he has acquired title by adverse possession.

Read the case file below as the first step in preparing for the negotiation. In addition to the case file, your professor will provide confidential information about the negotiation to each side. As you work on your negotiation plan: (1) consider how the elements of adverse possession are or are not met in light of the facts; and (2) use this legal analysis to justify your negotiating position.

ARCHER, KING & MARTINEZ

300 SOUTH GRAND AVENUE, 41ST FLOOR
CAPITAL CITY, MADISON 55480
792.899.2800 (PHONE)
792.899.2801 (FAX)
WWW.AKMLAW.COM

June 8, YR-00

Elmer G. Johnson
6009 West 45th Drive
Stovell, Madison 55419

SENT BY CERTIFIED MAIL
RETURN RECEIPT REQUESTED

Dear Mr. Johnson:

Our firm represents Laura M. Stone, the owner of a 20-acre tract of land located near Deep Spring, Madison. The land is shown as Lot 22 on the subdivision map of Deep Spring Estates, which was recorded on July 8, 1999, in Book 196, Page 45 of the El Dorado County land records (hereafter "Stone land"). I am enclosing a copy of the deed by which she obtained title.

We understand that you were present on the Stone land on April 23 of this year, where you met Ms. Stone. We further understand that on that occasion you claimed to be the owner of the Stone land. Ms. Stone has asked that we contact you to clarify what appears to be a misunderstanding.

As reflected in the second enclosed deed, you received title to a *different lot* in the same subdivision, Lot 21 (hereafter "Johnson land"), in 2004. The Johnson land is a 15-acre parcel which is immediately south of the Stone land; both adjoin Highway 86 to the east. You have never had any right, title, or interest in the Stone land. Apparently by mistake, you thought that you owned the Stone land, whereas in reality, your land is a different parcel, as shown on the enclosed map.

Ms. Stone has no interest in bringing any legal action against you based on your trespass onto her land. However, she requests that in the future you refrain from entering the Stone land unless she gives her prior consent. Of course, Ms. Stone will, in turn, refrain from entering your land.

Very truly yours,

Julia A. Fletcher

Julia A. Fletcher

9

Recording requested by:
Laura M. Stone
18 Wilshire Drive
Prairie City, Madison 55703

GRANT DEED

For valuable consideration, the receipt of which is hereby acknowledged, Tryon Development Corporation, a Madison corporation,   hereby grants to

Laura M. Stone

that certain real property in the County of   El Dorado,   State of Madison described as follows:

Lot 22 as shown on that certain subdivision map of Deep Spring Estates which was recorded on July 8, 1999 in Book 196, Page 45, El Dorado County Records

Dated: October 10, 1999   Signed: *Luisa De Cristo*

                                                    Executive Vice-President
                                                    Tryon Development Corporation

STATE OF MADISON
COUNTY OF   El Dorado

On   October 10, 1999   before me, the undersigned, a notary public in and for said State, personally appeared   Luisa De Cristo   personally known to me (or proved on the basis of satisfactory evidence) to be the person(s) whose name(s) is/are subscribed to the within instrument and acknowledged to me that he/she/they executed the same.

Signed: *Michael G. Parzen*

Deed for Jhonson

RECORDED

El Dorado County
Recorder's Office
10:56 am, 11/30/04
Book 203, Page 289

Recording requested by:
Elmer G. Johnson
6009 West 45th Drive
Stovell, Madison 55419

GRANT DEED

For valuable consideration, the receipt of which is hereby acknowledged, Tryon Development Corporation, a Madison corporation **hereby grants to** Elmer G. Johnson and his heirs

that certain real property in the County of El Dorado, **State of Madison described as follows:**

Lot 21 in Deep Spring Estates as shown on map recorded July 8, 1999, Book 196, Page 45, El Dorado County Records

Dated: November 29, 2004 **Signed:** *Luisa De Cristo*

Executive Vice-President
Tryon Development Corporation

STATE OF MADISON
COUNTY OF El Dorado

On November 29, 2004 **before me, the undersigned, a notary public in and for said State, personally appeared** Luisa De Cristo **personally known to me (or proved on the basis of satisfactory evidence) to be the person(s) whose name(s) is/are subscribed to the within instrument and acknowledged to me that he/she/they executed the same. Signed:** *Lena V. Lucherini*

Map of Stone and Johnson Parcels

Lot 22: 20-acre parcel owned by Stone

Highway 86

Lot 21: 15-acre parcel owned by Johnson

12

CHANG & SMITH
333 ELM STREET, SUITE 200
STOVELL, MADISON 55426
TEL (793) 376-4221
WWW.CHANGSMITH.COM

July 5, YR-00

Julia A. Fletcher, Esq.
Archer, King & Martinez
300 South Grand Avenue, 41st Floor
Capital City, Madison 55480

Dear Ms. Fletcher:

Our firm has been retained *represent* by Elmer F. Johnson, who has received your June 8 letter concerning his property located near Deep Spring, Madison, described as Lot 22 as shown on the subdivision map recorded on July 8, 1999, Book 196, Page 45, El Dorado County land records (hereafter "Lot 22").

Your letter correctly observes that the public land records do not reflect Mr. Johnson's title to Lot 22. However, Mr. Johnson has obtained title to this property by adverse possession. As you are undoubtedly aware, the period for adverse possession in Madison is five years. From 2004 through the present, a period of more than five years, Mr. Johnson has met all the requirements to obtain title to Lot 22 by adverse possession.

His activities have included camping on Lot 22 for an average of five days each summer, harvesting wild blueberries on the land, installing a plywood platform for his tent, and posting a metal "No Trespassing" sign. This conduct constituted actual possession. Mr. Johnson's possession was exclusive, in that neither your client nor anyone else used the land during this time. His possession was open and notorious as well; not only could anyone see him visibly using the land during his camping periods, but the tent platform and sign provided permanent, visible evidence of his claim to title. His possession was adverse and hostile under the majority view followed by Madison courts. Finally, his possession was as continuous as was required by the remote, unimproved nature of the land.

Under these circumstances, we ask your client to execute the enclosed quitclaim deed, formally conveying title to Mr. Johnson. Please return the signed deed to me for filing with the El Dorado County recorder's office, so that we can clarify the state of record title and thereby avoid any future confusion. Thank you for your anticipated cooperation in this matter.

Sincerely,

Robert T. Borland

Robert T. Borland

13

QUITCLAIM DEED

Laura M. Stone, an unmarried woman,   **hereby remises, releases, and quitclaims to**   Elmer F. Johnson, an unmarried man,   **that certain real property in the County of**   El Dorado, **State of Madison described as follows:**

Lot 22 as shown on the subdivision map of "Deep Spring Estates" recorded on July 8, 1999 in Book 196, Page 45, El Dorado County Records.

Dated:_____   Signed:_____

Laura M. Stone

STATE OF MADISON
COUNTY OF _____

On _____, before me, the undersigned, a notary public in and for said State, personally appeared   Laura M. Stone   personally known to me (or proved on the basis of satisfactory evidence) to be the person(s) whose name(s) is/are subscribed to the within instrument and acknowledged to me that he/she/they executed the same.

Signed: _____

ARCHER, KING & MARTINEZ
300 SOUTH GRAND AVENUE, 41ST FLOOR
CAPITAL CITY, MADISON 55480
792.899.2800 (PHONE)
792.899.2801 (FAX)
WWW.AKMLAW.COM

August 18, YR-00

Robert T. Borland, Esq.
Chang & Smith
333 Elm Street, Suite 200
Stovell, Madison 55426

Dear Mr. Borland:

In response to your July 5 letter in this matter, please be advised that Ms. Stone rejects the claim of your client that he has acquired title to Lot 22 by adverse possession. Accordingly, she will not execute the deed which was included in your letter.

Even under the most generous interpretation of the facts, your client has failed to satisfy a number of the elements required for adverse possession under Madison law. Camping and picking wild blueberries do not constitute actual possession of Lot 22, because a reasonable owner would use this land in a more intensive manner, given its character, location, and nature. Ms. Stone used the land for cross-country skiing from time to time, which means that the supposed possession of your client was not exclusive. Placing a piece of plywood and one small sign somewhere on 20 acres of very dense forest are inconspicuous acts that do not constitute open and notorious possession. Finally, being physically present on someone else's land for five days each year is not continuous possession, but rather a series of trespasses.

Moreover, any judge or jury would certainly be hostile to the effort of your client to, in effect, acquire *two* properties even though he only purchased *one* property. Your client intended to acquire one parcel, and he did successfully acquire title to one parcel: Lot 21. There is no logical reason for the law to deprive my client of title to her land *simply because your client made a mistake.*

Please inform me whether your client is now willing to acknowledge that Ms. Stone is the true owner of Lot 22 and to refrain from further trespassing. If this does not occur, we will file a quiet title action to clarify the state of title, a course of action which will require both sides to needlessly incur attorney's fees.

Very truly yours,

Julia A. Fletcher

Julia A. Fletcher

15

CHAPTER 2

GIFTS

A. INTRODUCTION

The exercise in this chapter involves the law of gifts of personal property. The concept of a legally-enforceable gift is universal. All legal systems recognize the right of an owner to give her property to another person. But the criteria for a valid gift vary widely among nations.

This exercise introduces the second main skill addressed in the book: advocacy. Every attorney is an advocate from time to time, whether in the courtroom or in a less formal setting, such as a casual discussion between attorneys whose clients have opposing positions in a business transaction. The advocate must be able to explain why the relevant facts in the case do or do not meet the applicable rule of law.

The first part of this chapter gives you an overview of the law of gifts. The second part introduces you to the skill of making a closing argument after a court trial. The final part is an advocacy exercise involving the law of gifts, based on a case file of documents. The exercise requires you to make a closing argument on behalf of your client in a lawsuit involving the alleged gift of a valuable meteorite.

B. OVERVIEW OF THE LAW

Tens of thousands of gifts are made every day in the United States. Almost always, no dispute arises. On the rare occasions when a dispute does occur, two conditions are usually present: (1) the item involved is particularly valuable (e.g., artwork or jewelry), which is why both sides have an incentive to litigate; and (2) the donor is dead, and thus unable to testify.

The law traditionally recognizes two categories of gifts: the inter vivos gift and the gift causa mortis. The *inter vivos gift* is an ordinary gift made between two living persons, such as a gift made at a birthday party or on a holiday. The *gift causa mortis* is also a gift between two living persons, but one which is motivated by a special reason: the donor's anticipation of imminent death from a particular peril. Why distinguish between the two types of gifts? The answer lies in revocation. An inter vivos gift is irrevocable. However, in most jurisdictions a gift causa mortis (1) may be revoked by the donor at any time before his death and (2) is automatically revoked if the donor does not die from the peril that motivated the gift.

The elements required for a valid inter vivos gift are intent, delivery, and acceptance:

1. *Intent:* The donor must intend to make an immediate transfer of his rights in the item to the donee. The necessary intent can be manifested by words, conduct, or other circumstances. At a birthday party, for example, the donor may show his intent by the words he uses (e.g., "This is a gift for you!"), by his conduct (e.g., placing the item where the donee directs), and by the circumstances (e.g., it is customary to give gifts on a person's birthday).

2. *Delivery:* The item must be delivered to the donee so that that the donor parts with dominion and control. The common law recognized three types of delivery: manual, constructive, and symbolic. *Manual delivery* occurs when the donor physically transfers possession of the item to the donee, such as where the donor hands a birthday present to the donee. The traditional rule is that constructive delivery or symbolic delivery may be used *only* if manual delivery is impossible or impracticable. Madison law follows the traditional view. *Constructive delivery* occurs when the donor physically transfers an object to the donee that provides a means of access to the gifted item. For example, suppose A wants to give a heavy desk to B; because of its weight, manual delivery would be impracticable. Under these circumstances, A can make a constructive delivery by handing B a key that opens the desk. *Symbolic delivery* occurs when the donor physically transfers to the donee an object that represents or symbolizes the gifted item. For example, suppose C wants to give D the copyright to a song. Because a copyright is intangible, manual delivery is impossible. C could deliver the copyright to D by giving him a letter reciting the fact of the gift because the letter symbolizes the gifted item. Alternatively, C might give D a copy of the sheet music to the song or a CD which contains the song.

3. *Acceptance:* The donee must accept the item. Acceptance may be manifested by the donee's words or conduct. At a birthday party, the donee's acceptance might be shown by her saying "Thank you!" to the donor or by physically taking the item from the donor. In addition, in most jurisdictions the law presumes that a valuable gift has been accepted. Madison follows this view. Thus, if the item is valuable, this element is satisfied—unless it can be shown that the donee rejected the gift.

A valid gift causa mortis has four essential elements: intent, delivery, and acceptance, as discussed above, and an additional element: the gift must be motivated by the *donor's anticipation of death from an imminent peril.* For example, suppose that E, suffering from terminal cancer, will surely die within a few days. Because she believes that death is imminent, E hands all of her jewelry to her best friend, F, saying: "Please take this jewelry as my gift." F replies: "I accept." On these facts, E has made a valid gift causa mortis to F. If E somehow recovers from her terminal cancer, the gift to F is automatically revoked.

C. CLOSING ARGUMENTS AFTER TRIAL

The exercise in this chapter is a closing argument in a lawsuit tried before a judge, without a jury. You will have the opportunity to give a closing statement in a jury trial in later exercises.

Why have a trial? A trial is necessary when there are *disputed issues of material fact*. If there are no disputed issues of material fact in a particular case, it can be decided relatively quickly by a judge as a matter of law. In this situation, one side will file a motion to dismiss or a motion for summary judgment, both sides will submit their legal arguments in written briefs, both sides will argue their positions before the judge in a short hearing (perhaps 10 to 20 minutes), and the judge will then decide the case.

Where there are disputed issues of material fact, the case may be decided by either a judge or a jury, depending on the circumstances. A *court trial* is a trial conducted by a judge, without a jury. In a court trial, each side makes a closing argument to the judge after the testimony is concluded. Each attorney will seek to demonstrate that the facts in the case do or do not meet the relevant legal standard. The facts used in a closing argument in a civil case mainly come from two sources. One source is the pleadings in the case. If the plaintiff's complaint and the defendant's answer agree on a particular fact, that fact may be used in argument. The more important source is the testimony received at the trial, including any exhibits admitted into evidence, and *reasonable inferences from those facts*. Often a particular fact cannot be proven directly. But an attorney may urge the court to draw an inference from facts which are proven. For example, suppose that G enters your law school classroom wearing a raincoat that drips water on the floor, and you hear the crash of thunder overhead as the door closes. On these facts, it is reasonable to infer that it is raining outside, even though you did not see the rain yourself.

D. *YEE v. OLDHAM*

The dispute in the exercise below is about who owns a valuable meteorite that was found by Blair Oldham; Oldham later died without leaving a will. Plaintiff Deborah Yee claims that Oldham gave her the meteorite as a gift; she sues in replevin to recover possession. The defendant is Terrence Oldham, Blair's adult son, who also claims title to the meteorite. If Blair Oldham owned the meteorite at the time he died, then it passed to Terrence Oldham, his closest relative, under the doctrine of intestate succession.

The trial testimony has concluded and closing arguments will occur after a short recess. Depending on what your professor decides, you may be the plaintiff's attorney, the defendant's attorney, or a judge in the case. As an attorney, your job is to explain why your client should prevail in the case, considering both the law and the facts.

For example, the attorney for the plaintiff will presumably argue that a valid inter vivos gift occurred. To do so, she must show why the evidence in the case demonstrates that the three elements of intent, delivery, and acceptance are present, based on the facts in evidence before the trial court and reasonable inferences from those facts. While the plaintiff's attorney must prove that all *three* elements are satisfied, notice that the defendant's attorney will win the case if he can show that any *one* of these three elements is missing. The defendant's attorney may want to argue, in the alternative, that if a gift was made, it was a gift causa mortis that was automatically revoked.

The case file below includes the complaint, the answer, and a partial transcript of the trial testimony. Both sides have access to the same facts.

Ford & Associates, LLP
224 San Juan Drive, Suite 7
Verano, Madison 55490
(793) 702-7401

September 18, YR-02

Mr. Terrence Oldham
981 North Elvira Street, Apt. 56B
Hazelhurst, Madison 55488

Dear Mr. Oldham:

My firm has been retained by Deborah Yee in connection with the meteorite which your father, Blair Oldham, found on approximately April 5, while walking on federal land. Under regulations promulgated by the U.S. Bureau of Land Management, he obtained ownership of the meteorite when he found it.

Subsequently, on April 9 your father gave the meteorite to my client during a meeting in his hospital room. He clearly expressed his intent that my client "have" the meteorite. Because the meteorite was potentially dangerous, and could not be moved without a special container, he was unable to make a manual delivery at that time. However, perhaps because he had some legal knowledge, he was able to meet the law's delivery requirement in a different manner. Finally, my client accepted the gift. Thus, all the legal requirements for a valid gift were satisfied on April 9, and Ms. Yee owned the meteorite at that time.

Perhaps you were unaware of these facts because you were estranged from Mr. Oldham. But, under these circumstances, when you apparently took the meteorite away following Mr. Oldham's tragic traffic accident, you were carrying away Ms. Yee's property, not your father's property. Accordingly, on behalf of my client I hereby demand that you return the meteorite to me within ten working days from the date of this letter. If you fail to do so, my client will have no choice but to file suit to recover the meteorite, with no further notice to you.

Please be advised that under Madison law you will be liable for conversion if you fail to return the meteorite as directed. Conversion is a tort which occurs when someone wrongfully interferes with the owner's title to, or right to possession of, personal property. When conversion occurs, the owner can recover both compensatory damages and punitive damages.

With best regards,

William T. Ford
William T. Ford

21

WILLIAM T. FORD
FORD & ASSOCIATES, LLP
224 San Juan Drive, Suite 7
Verano, Madison 55490
(793) 702-7401

Attorney for Plaintiff

SUPERIOR COURT OF MADISON

COUNTY OF TERRADO

DEBORAH M. YEE,

        Plaintiff,

vs.   NO. 83-157

TERRENCE S. OLDHAM,   COMPLAINT FOR REPLEVIN

        Defendant.

Plaintiff alleges as follows:

1. At all times herein mentioned, plaintiff DEBORAH M. YEE ("YEE") was an individual residing in Terrado County, Madison.

2. At all times herein mentioned, defendant TERRENCE S. OLDHAM ("OLDHAM") was an individual residing in Terrado County, Madison. OLDHAM is the son of Blair Oldam, who died intestate on May 10, YR-02.

3. On April 5, YR-02, Blair Oldham became the owner of a meteorite ("Meteorite"), blackish-grey in color, and weighing approximately 57 pounds, through the act of finding the Meteorite on federal land near Verano, Terrado County, Madison, in compliance with regulations issued by the U.S. Bureau of Land Management.

4. On April 9, YR-02, Blair Oldham made a valid gift of the Meteorite to YEE. Since that time, YEE has been the sole owner of the Meteorite and has been entitled to the immediate and exclusive possession of the Meteorite, except to the extent that she allowed possession to be temporarily held by another.

5. YEE allowed Blair Oldham to temporarily hold possession of the Meteorite between April 9 and May 10, YR-02. However, on May 10, YR-02, when Blair Oldham died, OLDHAM wrongfully and without YEE's consent took possession of the Meteorite. Since that time,

OLDHAM has been, and now is, in wrongful possession of the Meteorite in violation of YEE's right to immediate and exclusive possession. Through counsel, YEE has demanded that OLDHAM return the Meteorite to her, but OLDHAM has failed and refused to do so.

WHEREFORE, plaintiff prays for judgment as follows:

1. For possession of the Meteorite.

2. For costs of suit incurred herein.

3. For such other and further relief as the Court may deem proper.

Dated: November 25, YR-02   FORD & ASSOCIATES, LLP

By: *William T. Ford*
William T. Ford

ANDREA J. KRUSE
FENWICK, McCARTHY & GREEN
10 Wilmore Drive, Suite 500
Sparrow, Madison 55490
(793) 710-8800

Attorney for Defendant

SUPERIOR COURT OF MADISON

COUNTY OF TERRADO

DEBORAH M. YEE,

        Plaintiff,

vs.   NO. 83-157

TERRENCE S. OLDHAM,   ANSWER

        Defendant.

Defendant answers the Complaint filed herein as follows:

1. Defendant admits the allegations set forth in Paragraphs 1, 2, and 3.

2. Defendant denies each and every allegation set forth in Paragraph 4.

3. Answering the allegations set forth in Paragraph 5, defendant admits that Blair Oldham held possession of the Meteorite between April 9 and May 10, YR-02; that defendant took possession of the Meteorite when Blair Oldham died on May 10, YR-02; that defendant has held possession of the Meteorite since that time; that Yee has asked for possession of the Meteorite; and that defendant has refused this request. Except as expressly admitted above, defendant denies each and every remaining allegation set forth in Paragraph 5, and affirmatively alleges that defendant became the owner of the Meteorite by intestate succession when Blair Oldham died on May 10, YR-02.

WHEREFORE, defendant prays for judgment as follows:

1. That plaintiff take nothing by her complaint herein.

2. For costs of suit incurred herein.

3. For such other and further relief as the Court may deem proper.

Dated: December 23, YR-02   FENWICK, McCARTHY & GREEN

                         By: *Andrea J. Kruse*
                         Andrea J. Kruse

1 SUPERIOR COURT OF MADISON

2 COUNTY OF TERRADO

3 DEBORAH M. YEE,

4   Plaintiff,

5 vs.   NO. 83-157

6 TERRENCE S. OLDHAM,

7   Defendant.

8 EXCERPTS FROM TRIAL TRANSCRIPT

9 AUGUST 31, YR-00

10 BEFORE THE HONORABLE ARTHUR C. FANNIN

11 For the plaintiff: WILLIAM T. FORD, FORD & ASSOCIATES, LLP

12 For the defendant: ANDREA J. KRUSE, FENWICK, McCARTHY & GREEN

13 THE COURT: Before we begin, I understand that the parties have reached a stipulation

14 on certain matters. Is that correct?

15 KRUSE: Yes, your honor. In the interest of shortening the trial as much as possible, Mr.

16 Ford and I have stipulated as follows:

17 1. Blair Oldham discovered a meteorite weighing 57 pounds on April 5, YR-02 while he

18 was walking near Verano, Madison on federal land managed by the U.S. Bureau of Land

19 Management;

20 2. While running excitedly toward the meteorite, Mr. Oldham tripped and fell against a

21 rock, fracturing his skull;

22 3. Mr. Oldham was able to pick up the meteorite and place it in a large lead-lined box

23 which was in his possession before he called for help on his cell phone and fainted due to his

24 injury;

25 4. Pursuant to regulations adopted by the Bureau of Land Management, Mr. Oldham

26 acquired ownership of the meteorite by these actions;

27 5. The meteorite is admitted into evidence as Exhibit 1;

28 6. Mr. Oldham died intestate on May 10, YR-02 when he was struck by a bus;

29 7. At the time of Mr. Oldham's death, his only living relative was his son Terrence S.

30 Oldham, the defendant in this action;

1   8. If Mr. Oldham owned the meteorite at the time of his death, it passed by intestate

2   succession to the defendant, Terrence Oldham.

3   THE COURT: Mr. Ford, do you join in this stipulation?

4   FORD: Yes, your honor.

5   THE COURT: And Ms. Kruse, just to make sure, you also so stipulate?

6   KRUSE: Yes, your honor.

7   THE COURT: Then this stipulation of the parties is accepted. Now let me see if I

8   understand the situation. Mr. Ford, your client Ms. Yee alleges that she received the meteorite as

9   a gift from Mr. Oldham, the father, before he died, and accordingly that Terrence Oldham, the

10   son, could not have inherited it because his father did not own it when he died. Is that correct?

11   FORD: Yes, your honor. Exactly right.

12   THE COURT: Ms. Kruse, your client alleges that there never was a valid gift to Ms.

13   Yee, so the father still owned the meteorite when he died, and it passed to your client, his son, by

14   intestate succession. Is that correct?

15   KRUSE: Your honor, we do contend that there never was a valid inter vivos gift to Ms.

16   Yee. In addition, we contend that if any gift occurred, it was merely a gift causa mortis, which

17   was automatically revoked when Mr. Oldham failed to die from the head injury he suffered while

18   finding the meteorite.   Either way, Mr. Oldham still owned the meteorite when he died, so

19   ownership passed to my client.

20   *   *   *   *   *

21   THE COURT: Mr. Ford, you may call your first witness.

22   FORD: I call Deborah Yee.

23   DEBORAH M. YEE

24   called as a witness by the plaintiff, being first duly sworn, was examined and testified as follows:

25   DIRECT EXAMINATION

26   FORD: Would you state your full name for the record?

27   A. Deborah M. Yee. It's spelled Y-e-e.

28   Q. Ms. Yee, what is your occupation?

29   A. I'm a research scientist specializing in meteorites at the University of Madison Center

30   for Meteorite Analysis.   Most of my work involves high-resolution microscopic and

31   spectroscopic analysis of meteorites for the purpose of better understanding the solar system.

1   Q. Do you hold any professional degrees?

2   A. Yes. I received my B.S., M.S. and Ph.D. degrees in Astrogeology from the University

3   of Madison.

4   Q. Did you know Blair Oldham before his death?

5   A. Yes, I did.

6   Q. How did you come to know him?

7   A. He was a meteorite hunter, one of the best. I began purchasing meteorites for the

8   Center from Blair about seven years ago, and over time we became friends. He had an uncanny

9   ability to find or maybe just stumble across meteorites that were particularly rare. People think

10   that all meteorites are alike but they're not.

11   Q. When you say you became friends, what do you mean?

12   A. Well, we weren't what I would call close friends. But we had lunch together from

13   time to time and talked a lot about meteorites. We were both fascinated by them. You have to

14   understand that Blair didn't have many friends. Even Terry, his son, ignored him completely.

15   You would think that a son would want to be with his father, at least once in a while.

16   Q. To avoid confusion, when I ask about "Mr. Oldham," I will be asking about the father,

17   Blair Oldham. Is that all right with you?

18   A. Yes, of course.

19   Q. Did Mr. Oldham ever complain that his son was ignoring him?

20   KRUSE: Objection, your honor. Relevance. It's also hearsay.

21   FORD: Your honor, it goes to motivation, the intent to make a gift. We will establish

22   that Mr. Oldham didn't want his property to go to the defendant. This supports the view that he

23   intended it to go to my client.

24   THE COURT: Overruled. Proceed.

25   A. Yes, he certainly did. Blair once told me that when he died he didn't want Terry to get

26   anything from him. I guess you could say that they were estranged.

27   Q. Now did there come a time in April, YR-02 when you received a telephone call

28   concerning Mr. Oldham?

29   A. Yes, it was on April 9. I got a call from Doctor Vega, at Madison Memorial Hospital

30   who told me that Blair had been hospitalized there and wanted to see me. Blair had apparently

31   fallen and fractured his skull.

1   Q. Did Doctor Vega explain why Mr. Oldham wanted to see you?

2   KRUSE: Objection, your honor. That calls for hearsay.

3   THE COURT: Sustained. Move on, counsel.

4   FORD: What did you do, if anything, in response to that call?

5   A. I went over to the hospital that same day and met with Mr. Oldham.

6   Q. What happened during that meeting?

7   A. Well, Mr. Oldham had the meteorite there in his hospital room, in a box lined with

8 lead. It was the box he always used. That's a standard procedure used in handing certain types

9 of meteorites, those which may possibly emit harmful radiation, radiation that imperils human

10 health. And he told me that he wanted me to "have it," the meteorite.

11   Q. I now show you the object which has been admitted into evidence as Exhibit 1. Do

12 you recognize it?

13   A. Yes, that's the meteorite he gave me.

14   Q. As best you can recollect, exactly what did he say about wanting you to "have it"?

15   A. I can't remember the precise words he used. He said something along the lines that I

16 would be able to appreciate the scientific value of the meteorite, unlike Terry, so it made sense

17 that it should go to me under the circumstances, that I should "have it." He said that's why he

18 had asked me to come, so that I could have the meteorite.

19   Q. Did Mr. Oldham ask you to pay anything for the meteorite?

20   A. No.

21   Q. Did you leave the hospital with the meteorite?

22   A. No, I didn't.

23   Q. Why not?

24   A. At that point, we didn't know if it was dangerous, so it had to be kept in a lead box.

25 And I didn't have my own box with me, because I didn't know he was going to give me anything

26 before I came. So I left the meteorite in his room until I could return with my box.

27   Q. Did Mr. Oldham give you anything at all during that meeting?

28   A. Yes, he did and it was kind of strange. At one point, he opened the box briefly and

29 chipped off a minute fragment of the meteorite, weighing about one hundredth of a gram, and

30 handed it to me.

31   Q. Did he say anything when he handed it to you?

1   A. He said that "this would make it legal" or something like that.

2   Q. Did you understand what he meant by this at the time?

3   A. No.

4   Q. Where is that chip today?

5   A. It doesn't exist. I took it back to my lab to have it tested to determine if the meteorite

6 was emitting harmful radiation, and the chip was so tiny that it was destroyed during the testing

7 process.

8   Q. Did Mr. Oldham give you anything else on April 9?

9   A. He had a napkin left over from his lunch. He wrote on the napkin and handed it to me.

10   Q. What did the writing on the napkin say?

11   KRUSE: Objection, your honor. Under the best evidence rule, they should produce the

12 napkin, not testimony about what it supposedly said.

13   FORD: Your honor, unfortunately Ms. Yee didn't keep the napkin. All we can offer is

14 Ms. Yee's testimony.

15   THE COURT: I will allow the question.

16   A. On the napkin there was the word "meteorite," then there was an arrow which led to

17 the word "Debby."

18   Q. So the arrow connected the words "meteorite" and "Debby".

19   A. Yes.

20   Q. Who was "Debby"?

21   A. That was me. Blair always called me Debby.

22   Q. And did Mr. Oldham explain why he was giving you the napkin?

23   A. No.

24   Q. What did you do with the napkin?

25   A. I think I dropped it into a trash can as I left the hospital. It didn't make any sense to

26 me then.

27   Q. Did you ever obtain possession of the meteorite?

28   A. No. On April 10, YR-02, a very large meteorite fell in Chile, and I was sent down

29 there on an emergency basis. I didn't return until mid-May, after Blair had died. Terry had it,

30 the meteorite. I went to Terry's house on May 17 to get it, but he refused to give it to me.

31   Q. Did Terrence Oldham say anything else to you on that occasion?

1   A. Yes, he said that the meteorite was worth $500,000, and that he planned to "cash in"

2   on it.

3   Q. Based on your experience, was it worth that much?

4   A. Probably not, in my view. It was both large and rare, but I don't think anyone would

5   pay more than perhaps $425,000 for it.

6   Q. Did the testing show that the meteorite was in fact emitting harmful radiation?

7   A. No. It was completely benign. As it turned out, anyone could handle it without being

8   harmed. But we didn't know that at the time.

9   FORD: I have no further questions at this time.

10   THE COURT: Cross-examination?

11   CROSS-EXAMINATION

12   KRUSE: Thank you, your honor. Now Mr. Oldham didn't give you any meteorites

13 before April 9, YR-02, did he?

14   A. No.

15   Q. In fact, before that day, the only way you had acquired meteorites from him was by

16 buying them, isn't that right?

17   A. Yes, that's right.

18   Q. And isn't that the reason Mr. Oldham wanted to see you on that day—to sell you a

19 meteorite?

20   A. No, he wanted to give it to me.

21   Q. Why would Mr. Oldham suddenly want to give you a meteorite?

22   A. We were friends, of course. I think that being in the hospital reminded him that he

23 was mortal, that he wouldn't live forever. That's why he talked about not wanting Terry to get

24 the meteorite.

25   Q. Were there any witnesses to this supposed gift, anyone who overheard what Mr.

26 Oldham allegedly said to you?

27   A. I think Dr. Vega heard part of the conversation. That's all.

28   Q. Now let's turn to this supposed chip. I now show you Exhibit 1, the meteorite.

29 Please show the court the spot on Exhibit 1 where the chip came from.

30   A. I'm not sure. Every meteorite gets badly chipped as it falls to Earth.

31   Q. You're the only person who ever saw this chip, right?

1   A. Well, Blair did, of course. Other than that, yes. I did the testing on the chip myself.

2   Q. And you're the only person who ever saw this napkin, right?

3   A. Blair did, and I did.

4   KRUSE: I have nothing further at this time.

5   THE COURT: Mr. Ford, you may call your next witness.

6   FORD: Your honor, I call Dr. Alberto Vega.

7   <u>ALBERTO MARTINEZ VEGA</u>

8   called as a witness by the plaintiff, being first duly sworn, was examined and testified as follows:

9   <u>DIRECT EXAMINATION</u>

10   FORD: Please state your name and occupation for the record.

11   A. Sure. I'm Alberto Martinez Vega, and I'm a physician at Madison Memorial Hospital.

12   Q. Did you have any role in the treatment of Blair Oldham?

13   A. Yes, I did. I was the attending physician for Mr. Oldham while he was in the hospital

14   in April and May of YR-02.

15   Q. What was his condition as of April 9 of that year?

16   A. He had fractured his skull in three places. This was a serious injury, but in my view it

17   was probably not going to be fatal. I told Mr. Oldham the day he came in that he needed

18   surgery, but that there was about a 90% chance he would recover.

19   Q. What was his mental condition at that time? Was he competent to make decisions?

20   A. Yes, I would say so. He was alert. He understood the risks of surgery, and he

21   consented. Ultimately, the surgery was successful.

22   Q. Did Mr. Oldham ask you to call Deborah Yee and ask her to come to visit him in the

23   hospital?

24   A. Yes, he did, just after I told him he would probably recover.

25   Q. Why didn't he just call her himself?

26   A. I think he was afraid that she wouldn't come if he asked, that she would be more likely

27   to come if a doctor asked.

28   Q. And when she came, did you overhear any part of their conversation?

29   A. Not really. I know they were talking about the meteorite. I heard them mention that

30   several times. And they both seemed to be excited. Yes, and I think that Mr. Oldham may have

31   said something about its value.

1   Q. When Ms. Yee left the room, was she carrying anything?

2   A. Yes, she had a white object in her hand.

3   Q. Was it a napkin?

4   A. It could have been.

5   Q. Were you present when Mr. Oldham left the hospital on May 10, YR-02?

6   A. Yes, I walked out to the street with him. It was tragic.

7   Q. What was?

8   A. Well, he had made a successful recovery from the surgery. And he was carrying a

9 metal box, with the meteorite inside it. He was very excited about that meteorite, so excited that

10 as he crossed the street he didn't look carefully. He was hit by a bus and died on the spot. But

11 the meteorite wasn't harmed at all. His son Terrence later came to get it.

12   FORD: I have no further questions.

13   THE COURT: Ms. Kruse, do you wish to cross-examine?

14   <u>CROSS-EXAMINATION</u>

15   KRUSE: Yes, your honor. Dr. Vega, isn't it fair to say that as of April 9 there was a

16 substantial chance that Mr. Oldham would die from his injury?

17   A. Yes, I would say so.

18   Q. And in your experience, don't patients who face a substantial risk of death sometimes

19 want to give away their possessions?

20   FORD: Objection, your honor. It's beyond the scope of the direct.

21   THE COURT: Overruled. I'll allow it.

22   A. I don't really know. Maybe so.

23   Q. Now, I'm not clear about why Mr. Oldham wanted you to call Ms. Yee. Why didn't

24 he do it, if he was able?

25   A. I think he said they had had some sort of disagreement recently, a tiff. But he really

26 wanted her to come.

27   Q. Did he say anything to you about why he wanted her to come?

28   A. Just that she would be very excited about the meteorite.

29   Q. Didn't you overhear Mr. Oldham discuss the value of the meteorite with Ms. Yee

30 when they met on April 9?

1   A. Yes. He said something to the effect that it could be sold for lot of money. And she,

2   the plaintiff, she agreed with him that it was valuable.

3   Q. You didn't hear Mr. Oldham say that he wanted to give the meteorite to Ms. Yee or

4   words to that effect, did you?

5   A. No, but you have to understand that I was in and out. She was there for maybe 20

6   minutes, and I was within earshot for maybe 5 minutes during that time.

7   Q. You didn't see Mr. Oldham write anything on a napkin at that time, did you?

8   A. No. I did see a napkin in his room on a tray.

9   Q. You didn't see Mr. Oldham break a chunk off the meteorite and hand it to Ms. Yee,

10   did you?

11   A. No, I didn't. But there was a point during their meeting when I heard a loud sound in

12   or near his room, kind of a metallic clunk. I didn't know what that was.

13   KRUSE: Nothing further, your honor.

14   *   *   *   *   *

15   THE COURT: Ms. Kruse, you may call your first witness.

16   KRUSE: I call Terrence Oldham.

17   TERRENCE S. OLDHAM

18   called as a witness by the defendant, being first duly sworn, was examined and testified as

19   follows:

20   DIRECT EXAMINATION

21   KRUSE: Terry, please state your full name.

22   A. It's Terrence S. Oldham. O-l-d-h-a-m.

23   Q. And you were the son of Blair Oldham, now deceased?

24   A. Yes.

25   Q. In early April, YR-02, were you on good terms with your father?

26   A. That's hard to answer. We were getting along better than we had in the past, that's for

27   sure. I talked with him two or three times by phone while he was in the hospital.

28   Q. At that time, did you know he had found a large meteorite?

29   A. Yes, of course. He was very excited about it. It was the biggest one he had ever

30   found.

1   Q. Did he ever tell you that he intended to give that meteorite to anyone? Or that he had

2 given it away?

3   A. No. He just told me how valuable it was, how much money he could sell it for.

4   Q. When did he say that?

5   A. During various calls. I don't remember the times exactly.

6   Q. How much was your father's estate worth when he died?

7   A. In total, about $240,000, plus the value of the meteorite.

8   Q. Did your father ever tell you that he intended to disinherit you, to leave you nothing

9 when he died?

10   A. No, he certainly didn't. He would never have done that. Never.

11   KRUSE: That's all I have.

12   THE COURT: Any cross-examination?

13   CROSS-EXAMINATION

14   FORD: Yes, your honor. Mr. Oldham, you never visited your father while he was in the

15 hospital, did you?

16   A. No.

17   Q. And you didn't even come down to pick him up when he left the hospital, did you?

18   A. No. I think he planned to take a taxi.

19   Q. Isn't it true that the two of you were estranged?

20   A. No, that's not true at all.

21   Q. Isn't it true that your father had some legal training?

22   KRUSE: Objection. Beyond the scope of the direct.

23   THE COURT: Well, I let you have some latitude before. Overruled.

24   A. Yes. He had a master's degree in law. It was a one-year program at Madison

25 University Law School. He wasn't a lawyer, but he had studied law.

26   Q. And did he study property law during that program?

27   A. Yes, I think he did.

28   FORD: I have no further questions.

29   *   *   *   *   *

30   THE COURT: Now that both sides have rested, we will take a short recess. We'll

31 reconvene in 20 minutes for closing statements. Court is adjourned.

CHAPTER 3

ESTATES AND FUTURE INTERESTS

A. INTRODUCTION

The exercise in this chapter examines the topic of estates and future interests, which traditionally has been a major component of the first-year Property course. The American law governing estates and future interests was largely inherited from England. This English law was the product of political, economic, and social forces that spanned centuries. Over time, American courts and legislatures somewhat simplified the law in this area—but it remains confusing even today.

This is a negotiation exercise which arises out of the potential sale of a restaurant. You will act as an attorney for either the buyer or the seller in trying to negotiate a successful transaction, despite a possible problem with the seller's title to the restaurant property. It appears that the deed to the seller conveyed a fee simple defeasible, not a fee simple absolute.

The first part of this chapter is a brief overview of defeasible estates and the future interests that accompany them. The next part provides you with two new techniques to use in the negotiation. The last part is a case file containing the documents relevant to the transaction.

B. OVERVIEW OF THE LAW

Every estate in land is either absolute or defeasible. A *defeasible fee simple* is a fee simple estate which may continue forever *or* may end when a particular future event occurs. For example, suppose that O grants "to A and her heirs for so long as A refrains from smoking." This language creates a defeasible estate. If A refrains from smoking during her lifetime, the duration of the estate is potentially infinite. On the other hand, if A smokes, then A's estate will end. Notice that at the time A's estate is created, it is impossible to know which alternative will happen.

There are three types of defeasible fee simple estates: (1) the fee simple determinable; (2) the fee simple subject to a condition subsequent; and (3) the fee simple subject to an executory limitation. In the exercise below, the future interest following the estate was retained by the transferor. Accordingly, the traditional rule is that the estate must be one of the first two types: either a fee simple determinable or a fee simple subject to a condition subsequent. How can we distinguish between these two estates?

1. *Fee simple determinable:* The fee simple determinable *automatically* ends when a specified event or condition occurs, immediately giving the right to possession to the original transferor. This estate is characterized

by words of time or duration, such as *while, during,* and *so long as.* The future interest which accompanies this estate is the *possibility of reverter.*

2. *Fee simple subject to a condition subsequent:* The fee simple subject to a condition subsequent does not end automatically. Rather, when the specified condition or event occurs, the transferor has the *option* of taking action to terminate the estate, which he may or may not do. This estate is characterized by words that permit the transferor to retake possession, such as *provided that, but if,* and *on condition that.* The future interest which accompanies this estate is commonly called a *right of entry.* In some states, it is known as a *right of reentry* and in others as a *power of termination.*

Despite this theoretical clarity, it can often be difficult in practice to determine which estate is created by ambiguous language in a grant or devise. For example, the leading case of *Mahrenholz v. County Board of School Trustees of Lawrence County,* 417 N.E.2d 138 (Ill. App. Ct. 1981), involved the grant of a parcel of land to a school district that provided: "this land to be used for school purpose only; otherwise to revert to Grantors herein." At the time, Illinois followed the general national rule that where ambiguous language was used in creating a defeasible fee simple, it would be construed to be a fee simple subject to a condition subsequent. But, finding that the granting language was not ambiguous, the court held that it created a fee simple determinable. It reasoned that the word "only" contained an implied time limitation: the grantors "wanted to give the land to the school district only as long as it was needed and no longer." *Id.* at 142. In addition, the phrase "otherwise to revert to Grantors herein" seemed to the court to "trigger a mandatory return rather than a permissive return . . . ." *Id.* at 143.

Three additional aspects of the law governing defeasible fee simple estates merit special note:

1. *Transfers:* The modern rule is that these estates and their accompanying future interests can be alienated, devised, and transferred by intestate succession. For example, suppose again that O grants "to A and her heirs for so long as A refrains from smoking." A has a fee simple determinable, which she can transfer to B; O has a possibility of reverter, which he can transfer to P.

2. *Terminology:* The names of these estates and future interests do not change if they are transferred to new holders. Thus, in the hypothetical above, assuming that A transfers to B, B's estate is still called a fee simple determinable; similarly, the future interest which P receives from O is still called a possibility of reverter.

3. *Interpretation of defeasible language:* An old legal maxim says that "equity abhors a forfeiture." Accordingly, courts tend to interpret defeasible language narrowly, in order to prevent the owner from losing her estate. It is important to remember this constructional preference when dealing with a defeasible estate. For example, in a later installment of the *Mahrenholz* saga, an Illinois court ruled that the use of the land to store

school equipment was a use for "school purpose," even though no classes were being conducted on the property. Accordingly, the court held that the school district did not lose title to the land.

So why does the distinction between these defeasible estates matter? Two of the more important reasons are:

1. *Rents:* If the estate is a fee simple determinable and the event or condition occurs, the future interest holder automatically receives the right of possession. If the former estate owner remains in possession, he is liable to the new owner for the rental value of the property. Conversely, because the fee simple subject to a condition subsequent does not end automatically, the estate continues until the future interest holder acts; until that occurs, the estate holder is entitled to possession and owes no rent.

2. *Adverse possession:* In all states, the period for adverse possession begins running as soon as a fee simple determinable ends. When the estate is a fee simple subject to a condition subsequent, however, the law is less clear. Logically, when the triggering event or condition occurs in a fee simple subject to a condition subsequent, this period should not begin to run until the future interest holder takes action to end the estate. However, in some states the period begins running when the future interest holder has the right to end the estate, even if she has not yet exercised that right. Madison courts have not yet decided when the adverse possession period begins running in the case of a fee simple subject to a condition subsequent.

C. NEGOTIATION TECHNIQUES

Two negotiation techniques were discussed in Chapter 1:

1. *Develop a plan for the negotiation.*

2. *Set appropriate goals for the negotiation.*

This section will introduce you to two additional techniques.

3. *Envision the negotiation from the other side's perspective:* A good negotiator has the ability to think about the negotiation from the perspective of the other side. As you develop your plan for the negotiation, you should consider what your opponents intend to do. What are the strengths and weaknesses they see in their own position? In your position? What will their strategy be in the negotiation? Use this information in crafting your plan.

4. *Develop two goals: an aspirational goal and a bottom-line goal:* Many attorneys enter into a negotiation with one goal in mind: the bottom line. An attorney representing the seller in negotiating the sale of land, for example, probably has in mind the minimum amount that her client is willing to take for the property. At the same time, the attorney hopes to negotiate a higher price than the minimum. You should certainly establish a bottom-line goal. But you should also establish an aspirational goal—a specific outcome for the client that is significantly better than the

bottom-line goal and potentially achievable. Empirical research demonstrates that negotiators who have both types of goals in mind tend to be more successful. Perhaps this is because having a specific aspirational goal gives them a target to work toward.

D. THE SALE OF "FINN'S PLACE"

In this simulation, Oliver Finn owns "Finn's Place," a successful fish restaurant in Madison. Finn also owns the property on which it is located. Finn has been discussing the sale of the restaurant and property with Jessica Warner, a long-time customer. Tentative discussions between the parties were proceeding well, until Warner's attorney examined title to the restaurant property and learned that Finn has a defeasible fee simple, not a fee simple absolute. In this negotiation, you will be an attorney representing Finn or an attorney representing Warner.

The negotiation raises some challenging issues. Should an attorney ever counsel a client to purchase a defeasible fee simple estate? If so, under what terms and conditions? You will find that the above overview of the law governing defeasible estates is helpful in the exercise.

Read the case file below as the first step in preparing for the negotiation. In addition to the file, your professor will provide you with confidential information concerning your side of the negotiation. As you work on your negotiation plan, be sure to consider: (1) Is it more likely that a court would view Finn's estate as a fee simple determinable or a fee simple subject to a condition subsequent?; (2) How narrowly would a court interpret the defeasible language?; and (3) Is the adverse possession doctrine relevant?

Finn's Place
"Finest Fish in the City!"
**350 South Broadway
Metropolis, Madison 55901
(790) 753-9907
www.FinnsPlace.com**

October 3, YR-00

Ms. Jessica B. Warner
18 Waterfront Lane
Marmot, Madison 55807

Dear Jessie:

It was a pleasure to meet with you last night about Finn's Place. Running it has literally been the center of my life for more than 20 years, and while I have loved the experience, retirement beckons at long last. I was delighted to learn that you seem to value Finn's Place almost as much as I do. At least you're a long-time customer, which says a lot for your judgment.

It's always iffy to start a new business, particularly a restaurant. Even with Finn's Place, there were times in the early days when I wasn't sure we would make it work. There are so many fine fish restaurants in the city, so much competition. But when a restaurant has been around as long as mine has, it has usually established a solid customer base and a good reputation. As you know, Zagat continues to give us a favorable rating and even the comments on Yelp are reasonably good, though Yelp tends to attract a younger crowd who sometimes don't appreciate fine fish. What I mean by all this is that if you're serious about owning a restaurant, you're better off buying an established business like mine rather than trying to start from scratch.

Now I know we don't have any deal yet, even though you talked like we did. Maybe you had too much of that free wine. But I thought we got very close to an understanding yesterday. You will want to do your due diligence, of course, and run this all by your lawyer to make sure it's right for you. If we go ahead, I don't want you to have any second thoughts about the deal later. Both of us have to be happy with it.

I'm afraid that note we wrote the possible deal points on was later accidentally placed on a wet spot on the salad counter, so it's not very legible, but I'm enclosing a copy anyway. So here is the framework we were talking about. The sales price would be $1,250,000 in cash, paid directly to me. I know it's old fashioned, but I own the business and the restaurant building and land as an individual, not as a corporation. In return, you would receive all my rights in the business, however the lawyers define this, but it would certainly include the equipment, inventory, fixtures, accounts receivable, good will, trademarks, and so forth. You would also receive title to the restaurant building and land. Most restaurants operate in leased premises. One of the big advantages to buying my operation is that you would be the owner of the building and land, without having to worry about a landlord. Before the sale closes, I would work with you and your new manager for a period of weeks to bring both of you up to speed on the operation—suppliers, discounts, personnel, insurance, utilities, bookkeeping, etc. Of course, the deal would have to be written up by the attorneys in a comprehensive sales agreement, to protect both of us, and we would both have to sign it before we were bound to any deal.

The free wine has been a big part of our success. So many nights folks are standing like sardines (no pun intended) in that little waiting area just inside the front doors. But with some wine in them, most of them don't seem to mind the wait. I get the wine at quite a good price, so the cost to me works out to only $.25 per glass. And what a difference it makes! I don't really know why other restaurants don't do this. Maybe they think it will cut into their wine sales at dinner. But that really doesn't affect us, as you know, because we don't sell any wine at all.

If you're still interested in making this deal, why don't you go to your lawyer and get the ball rolling. The lawyer I would use for this is Angie Micheli, who does all of the work for Finn's Place. I think you and I know the key points of the deal. If your lawyer can put together a formal agreement on this basis, have him send it over to Angie for review, and we'll see if this can happen.

I just want to say that you would have a wonderful experience being the owner of Finn's Place. And I would feel good that I had passed it on to someone who really cared for it. It's always been more than a business to me, more like a sort of social club.

Sincerely,

Ollie

Oliver Finn

Jessie's dream busine

Terms of possible deal, wi
committed to anything yet

Free wine!!!!

$1,250,000 cash to me

Jessie gets business and land, everyt

Lawyers will document deal, in formal agreeme

I help with transition before retiring

October 7

Ollie:

Many thanks for your letter. Yes, it would be a dream come true if I could become the owner of Finn's Place. I have loved the place since I first ate there, more than ten years ago. But as I think about it, the price we discussed tentatively seems high. I really don't know much about buying restaurants, of course, but it seems high.

The other thing I wanted to ask about was the free wine. Some of the other restaurants on the same block don't serve wine, or even beer, nothing alcoholic at all. If the free wine is so important to the success of Finn's Place, what would happen if those other restaurants decided to start serving wine, too? Wouldn't that mean that the business of Finn's Place would suffer? So, if I bought the place and that happened, I would be stuck. I don't understand why all the restaurants in the area don't give away free wine. Maybe they don't have a permit from the Madison Alcoholic Beverage Authority?

Anyway, I am planning to meet with Scott Harada at Miller & Harada, who will help me with this deal. You should be hearing from him soon.

Cheers,
Jessie

42

301 PARK STREET, SECOND FLOOR
METROPOLIS, MADISON 55912
TEL (792) 376-4221
WWW.MILLERHARADA.COM

October 15, YR-00

Angela B. Micheli, Esq.
Cooley, DeVere & Smythe
18 Founders Plaza, Suite 1100
Metropolis, Madison 55912

Dear Ms. Micheli:

Our firm represents Jessica B. Warner, who has been negotiating with your client Oliver X. Finn concerning her possible purchase of the restaurant commonly known as "Finn's Place." We understand that Mr. Finn operated the restaurant profitably for many years and finally decided to retire. Our clients had tentatively discussed the idea that Ms. Warner would purchase the restaurant (including the real property, together with its fixtures, equipment, inventory, accounts receivable, trademarks, trade secrets, good will, and all other items of personal property in any way associated with the operation of the restaurant) for the sum of $1,250,000. However, no binding agreement was reached between the parties.

We have now learned that there appears to be a serious defect in your client's title to the real property on which the restaurant is operated. I am enclosing a copy of the 1988 deed by which your client obtained title to the property from its prior owner, Alberta F. Simony. The deed makes it clear that your client does not hold a fee simple absolute in the land. Instead, he merely has a defeasible fee simple, the restriction being that alcohol may not be "sold" on the property. Your client did not disclose this title problem to Ms. Warner.

One reason for the success of "Finn's Place" is that for many years patrons waiting to be seated in the restaurant have been given glasses of "free" white wine by Mr. Finn and his employees, which they normally consume while standing in the small waiting area. Indeed, on a busy evening, at any one time there may be as many as 30 patrons in the waiting area, most of them drinking wine. If this practice of giving wine to waiting patrons could be construed as a "sale" of alcohol, then it would appear that your client's title to the property could be in jeopardy and, accordingly, we could not recommend to our client that she continue with this transaction under the terms which are currently contemplated. Is your client in a position to assure Ms. Warner that there is no possibility whatsoever that any court would find a defect in his title to the restaurant property? If so, how?

Sincerely,

Scott B. Harada
Scott B. Harada

Recording requested by:
Oliver X. Finn
122 Lakecliff Drive
Metropolis, Madison 55901

GRANT DEED

Alberta F. Simony, an unmarried woman, **hereby grants to**

Oliver X. Finn, an unmarried man, so long as alcohol is not sold on the property, and if alcohol is sold on the property, the grantor reserves the right to re-enter the property and re-take possession,

that certain real property in the County of   Fremont,   **State of Madison described as follows:**

Lot 12A, as shown on that certain subdivision map of "Richmond Heights Estates," recorded on April 7, 1923 at Book 42, Page 73, Fremont County Records

Dated: June 11, 1988   **Signed:**   *Alberta A. Simony*

Alberta F. Simony

STATE OF MADISON
COUNTY OF Fremont

On June 11, 1988   **before me, the undersigned,**
a notary public in and for said State, personally
appeared   Alberta F. Simony   **personally known**
to me (or proved on the basis of satisfactory
evidence) to be the person(s) whose name(s)
is/are subscribed to the within instrument and
acknowledged to me that he/she/they executed
the same.

Signed: *Hazel O. Jachens*

COOLEY, DeVERE & SMYTHE
18 FOUNDERS PLAZA, SUITE 1100
METROPOLIS, MADISON 55912
(792) 889-3910
WWW.COOLDEV.COM

November 3, YR-00

Scott B. Harada, Esq.
Miller & Harada
301 Park Street, Second Floor
Metropolis, Madison 55912

Dear Mr. Harada:

Thank you for your letter of October 15 concerning the sale of "Finn's Place." You are correct that our firm represents Mr. Finn in this matter, and we hope that it will be possible to work out a successful sale to your client Ms. Warner.

Let me assure you that Mr. Finn holds good title to the restaurant property, without any risk that it might be lost. First, Finn's Place has never "sold" wine. Rather, wine has been given away freely to potential patrons waiting for a table. On a few occasions, a customer who has received the free wine has left the restaurant without eating, usually because the wait is too long; no one from Finn's Place has ever demanded any payment in this situation. Moreover, the original grantor, Alberta F. Simony, visited the restaurant on two or three occasions between 1988 and her unfortunate death last year. At no time did she ever object to the fact that free glasses of wine were given to people waiting for tables.

Second, even if it could somehow be argued that giving away free wine was inconsistent with the terms of the deed, my client Mr. Finn acquired title to the restaurant property by adverse possession; you will recall that the adverse possession period in Madison is only five years.

Finally, Ms. Simony died intestate last year. Her only living relative is a nephew, one William Simony, who is a citizen of New Zealand and has never visited the United States. Presumably the estate of Ms. Simony passed to Mr. Simony by intestate succession, including any conceivable claim under the deed. But there is no reason in the world to believe that he would raise any objection to this situation, just as his aunt did not complain. In fact, Mr. Simony probably does not even know that he is the heir to the estate.

Under these circumstances, we believe that the original sales price for the restaurant is still appropriate. Our client stands ready to finalize the sales transaction on this basis.

Very truly yours,

Angela B. Micheli
Angela B. Micheli

CHAPTER 4

CONCURRENT OWNERSHIP

A. INTRODUCTION

The exercise in this chapter explores the *tenancy in common,* a form of concurrent ownership. The key characteristic of concurrent ownership is that each cotenant has the right to use and possess the entire property. But what happens if the cotenants disagree about how to use the property? All states have developed default rules that establish the rights and duties of cotenants in this situation.

This is a negotiation exercise which arises out of a dispute among three siblings concerning the house that was left to them under their father's will. You will act as an attorney for one or more of the siblings in trying to negotiate a mutually-agreeable solution to the dispute.

The first section of the chapter is a short overview of the relevant law governing concurrent ownership. It is followed by a section that gives you two new techniques to use in the negotiation. The final section is the case file of documents relevant to the dispute.

B. OVERVIEW OF THE LAW

Modern law recognizes three basic types of concurrent ownership: the *tenancy in common,* the *joint tenancy,* and the *tenancy by the entirety.* Any grant or devise to two or more persons is generally presumed to create a tenancy in common, unless (1) there is clear intent to create another cotenancy and (2) the special requirements for that cotenancy are satisfied. Thus, the tenancy in common is the simplest form of cotenancy.

Three aspects of the law governing tenancies in common deserve special mention:

1. *Liability for rent:* In a tenancy in common, each cotenant holds an undivided, fractional interest in the entire property. For example, A and B might each own a ½ share in a farm. Each cotenant also has the right to use and possess that property. Accordingly, the majority view is that a cotenant who is in possession of cotenancy property does not owe any rent to a cotenant out of possession, absent an ouster. Thus, if only A is in possession of the farm, A owes no rent to B unless A ousts B. An *ouster* occurs when a cotenant in possession refuses to allow another cotenant to occupy the property. If an ouster occurs, the cotenant in possession is liable to the ousted cotenant for that cotenant's pro rata share of the rental value of the property. If the fair rental value of the farm is $4,000 per month and A ousts B, then A is liable to B for half of this amount, or $2,000 per month.

2. *Liability for expenses:* The general rule is that each cotenant must pay his proportional share of mortgage payments, real estate taxes, insurance costs, and similar payments that could give rise to a lien against the property if they were left unpaid. However, expenditures for repairs and improvements are treated differently. The majority view is that a cotenant who pays for repairs has no right to collect from other cotenants. However, if the property is later partitioned (see discussion below) or an accounting action is brought because rents or profits have been received from third parties, the cotenant who paid for reasonable repairs receives a credit for that expense. Similarly, a cotenant who pays for improvements to the property (e.g., a new roof or swimming pool) has no right to collect from other cotenants. But if the property is later partitioned or an accounting action is brought, the cotenant who paid for the improvement receives a credit equal to the amount by which the improvement enhanced the fair market value of the property.

3. *Partition:* Conflicts often arise among cotenants. For example, if A and B are cotenants in a farm, they may disagree about how it should be managed or whether it should be sold to a developer. The common law developed an easy escape hatch from such a situation. Any cotenant has the right to sue for judicial *partition* of the property, which ends the cotenancy. There is no need for the cotenant to prove fault or establish any special justification; rather, a court will automatically grant partition if it is requested by any cotenant. Thus, in partition actions, the issue is not *whether* partition will occur, but rather *how* it will occur. There are two types of partition: *partition in kind* and *partition by sale*. Partition in kind is a physical division of the property into different parcels. If partition in kind is used in the A-B example, A will receive sole title to half of the farm, while B receives sole title to the other half. In general, partition in kind is the preferred remedy. However, if partition in kind is impracticable or inequitable, the court has the discretion to order partition by sale. In this form of partition, the property is sold and the sales proceeds are divided between the cotenants on a pro rata basis. For example, if the A-B farm sells for $600,000, A and B would each receive $300,000.

C. NEGOTIATION TECHNIQUES

You learned four negotiation techniques in earlier chapters:

1. *Develop a plan for the negotiation.*

2. *Set appropriate goals for the negotiation.*

3. *Envision the negotiation from the other side's perspective.*

4. *Develop two goals: an aspirational goal and a bottom-line goal.*

This section will briefly introduce you to two additional techniques.

5. *Ask questions:* You will be a better negotiator if you understand the other side's position. The negotiation provides a forum for you to learn more about the other side by asking questions. Research suggests that good negotiators ask twice as many questions as the average negotiator.

Your questions should be open-ended so that the other side has an opportunity to talk (e.g., Why? What? How?), not questions that call for a yes or no answer. Why does it help to ask questions? First, the answers may provide you with information that you can use to your client's advantage during the negotiation. Second, if your opponent has difficulty answering one or more of your questions, he may conclude that his position on the point is weaker than he initially thought, which may lead him to alter his stance in the negotiation.

6. *Revisit the plan:* After each exercise, compare (a) your plan for the negotiation with (b) what actually happened. Consider the strengths of your plan and the areas where it could have been improved. Use the insights you derive from this process as you formulate negotiation plans in the future.

D. THE FURMANI FAMILY HOME

The clients in this exercise are the children of Elbert Furmani, who died a few years ago. His will left the family home to his three children as tenants in common. One of the children, Robert Furmani, has been living in the home without paying any rent. His siblings, Melissa Howard and Harold Furmani, live elsewhere in the same town. At some point, Melissa and Harold stop making their share of payments for the mortgage debt and other expenses, and the bank begins foreclosure proceedings. Eventually, Melissa and Harold demand partition. In this exercise, the attorneys for the parties will meet to try to resolve all the outstanding disputes. You will be an attorney in the negotiation representing either (1) Robert or (2) Melissa and Harold.

Begin your preparation for the negotiation by reading the case file below. In addition to the file, your professor will provide you with confidential information concerning your side of the negotiation. As you develop your negotiation plan, be sure to consider: (1) Is Robert liable for rent?; (2) Are Melissa and Harold liable for any share of the expenditures made by Robert?; and (3) Will a court grant partition by sale?

August 31, YR-01

Dear Bob:

Since you now refuse to talk to us, we are sending you this letter in an effort to clear the air. Ever since dad died, you have been living in the house without paying any rent, while we have to pay two-thirds of the mortgage, tax, and insurance costs, without receiving any benefit from the house. And the cottage is full of your stuff, so we can't rent that out.

This just isn't fair. You know that we have to support our own families, and we are barely getting by in this tough economy. Jill has even had to take a second job, on top of her job at Safeway. We can't afford to subsidize your living in the house, particularly after you refused to let even your own nephews move in to live there. The house is the only big asset dad left us, and each of us is entitled to one-third of its value, including its rental value. We figure that similar houses probably rent for $3,000 per month. Since you refuse to let us use the place at all, you should pay us $2,000 per month, representing our two-thirds share. If you refuse to do this, we will have to stop paying the mortgage and other costs. We can't afford to make these payments.

Bob, you are our brother and we love you. We know you don't have much money, and we are as sympathetic as we can be about your disability. We honor your service to our country. But financially we just can't let this situation go on. So tell us what you think would be fair. We think the best outcome would be to have you move out, so we can sell the house and split the proceeds equally.

Love,

Melissa

Harry

Madison Veterans Legal Center
1276 East Lincoln Boulevard, Suite 19
Capital City, Madison 55481
(792) 899-2341

Honoring our nation's heroes

August 10, YR-00

Melissa Howard
582 Norwalk Drive, Apt. 3C
Esperanza, Madison 55607

Harold Furmani
89 Water Street, Apt. 2
Esperanza, Madison 55607

Dear Mrs. Howard and Mr. Furmani:

I am an attorney representing your brother, Robert Furmani. As I understand the situation, your father Elbert Furmani died a few years ago. At that time, he was the owner of a single-family home located at 1032 Springdale Road in Esperanza. When the probate of your father's will was completed, the two of you and Robert each received a one-third interest in the home, in what the law calls a tenancy in common. A copy of the will is enclosed.

As tenants in common, each of you owes certain duties and responsibilities to the others concerning the home. One of these obligations is to share in making the payments that are necessary to preserve the property. Since you stopped making your share of these payments last October, my client has had to pay them out of his savings. In the past eleven months, he has made the following payments: (a) mortgage: $7,381 ($671 per month); (b) insurance: $2,332 ($212 per month); (c) property taxes: $3,004 (annual payment); and (d) roof repairs: $12,911 (one-time payment). This is a total of $25,628 in payments. Each of you owes my client one-third of this amount, or $8,543. In addition, you are required to pay your respective shares of the regular expenses in a timely manner.

Our center provides free legal assistance to veterans in need like your brother. Because he is effectively paying your shares of the expenses, as well as his own, his savings are almost gone. Due to the injury to his hand, the types of jobs which he can get are quite limited, and his income is not high enough to cover all these costs. Accordingly, I implore you to comply with your legal obligations to him.

Sincerely,

Kathleen B. Lawrence

Kathleen B. Lawrence
Attorney

WILL OF
ELBERT ROBERT FURMANI

I, Elbert Robert Furmani, a resident of Lancaster County, Madison, declare that this is my will. I hereby revoke all my previous wills and codicils.

Article 1: Introductory Provisions

1.01 <u>Marital Status</u>: I am not currently married. I was previously married to Eleanor Baines Furmani, who died on December 3, 2005.

1.02 <u>Identification of Living Children</u>: I have three living children, whose names and dates of birth are as follows: Robert Henry Furmani, who was born on January 11, 1965; Melissa Beth Furmani, now known as Melissa Beth Howard, who was born on June 27, 1968; and Harold Elbert Furmani, who was born on October 20, 1971.

Article 2: Disposition of Estate

2.01 <u>Disposition of Real Property</u>: I hereby devise my real property located at 1032 Springdale Road, Esperanza, Madison, to my three children, Robert Henry Furmani, Melissa Beth Howard, and Harold Elbert Furmani, as tenants in common, each such child to receive a one-third share in said property.

2.02 <u>Disposition of Ford</u>: I hereby bequeath my beloved 1965 Ford Mustang to my son Robert Henry Furmani.

2.03 <u>Disposition of Residue</u>: I hereby devise and bequeath the residue of my estate to my three children, Robert Henry Furmani, Melissa Beth Howard, and Harold Elbert Furmani, in equal shares.

Article 3: Executor

3.01 <u>Nomination of Executor</u>: I hereby nominate my son Robert Henry Furmani as the executor of this will. If he is for any reason unable or unwilling to serve as executor, I nominate Esperanza Bank & Trust Company as successor executor.

3.02 <u>Bond</u>: No bond shall be required of any executor of this will.

3.03 <u>Powers of Executor</u>: The executor shall have, in addition to all of the powers now or hereafter conferred upon executors by law, the power to perform any of the acts set forth below:

(a) Take possession or control of all of my estate subject to disposition by this will, and collect all debts due to me or to my estate;

(b) Receive the rents, issues, and profits from all real and personal property in my estate until the estate is settled or delivered over by order of court to my heirs or beneficiaries;

(c) Take all other steps reasonably necessary for the management, protection, and preservation of all property in my estate.

3.04 Executor's Liability: The executor shall not be liable to my estate or to any person interested in it for any act or omission of the executor, except for an act or omission that is committed intentionally or in bad faith, or an act or omission from which the executor derives a profit.

Article 4: Concluding Provisions

4.01 No-Contest Clause: If any beneficiary under this will challenges the validity of this will on any ground whatsoever, then the right of that person to take any gift or other interest given to him or her by this will shall be void, and any gift or other interest in my estate to which the person would have otherwise been entitled shall pass to the American Cancer Society.

4.02 Intentional Omission: Except as otherwise provided for in this will, I have intentionally and with full knowledge omitted to provide for any heirs, whether or not I am aware of their existence and identities at the time this will is executed.

4.03 Madison Law: All questions concerning the validity and interpretation of this will shall be governed by Madison law.

Executed on November 22, 2007, at Esperanza, Madison.

Elbert Robert Furmani

Elbert Robert Furmani

On the date written above, we, the undersigned, each being present at the same time, witnessed the signing of this will by Elbert Robert Furmani.

Dated: November 22, 2007   *Michelle A. Kalina*
                                         witness

Dated: November 22, 2007   *Joshua W. Cottrell*
                                         witness

MUIR & WINSTON
ATTORNEYS AT LAW
802 MARKET STREET
ESPERANZA, MADISON 55607
(792) 890-0337

September 18, YR-00

Kathleen B. Lawrence, Esq.
Madison Veterans Legal Center
1276 East Lincoln Blvd., Suite 19
Capital City, Madison 55481

Dear Ms. Lawrence:

Melissa Howard and Harold Furmani have retained me to represent them in connection with the dispute over the family home with their brother Robert. I would like to take this opportunity to respond to your August 10 letter.

First, my clients are extremely sympathetic to Robert's financial situation. They love him and want to help him as much as they can. But the reality is that Robert is living in a house worth perhaps $350,000, paying no rent to my clients, and refusing to compromise in any way. My clients are working people, living in rented apartments; they are barely making enough money at their jobs to survive. Their shares in the home are the biggest assets they have. But because of Robert's intransigence, they are not receiving any benefit from it. They cannot afford to keep paying the mortgage and other costs.

Second, the fact is that my clients attempted to use the family home thirteen months ago by having their family members move in—Melissa's son Sam and Harold's son Brett. There are five bedrooms in the home, plenty of room for Robert to share space with his nephews. But when Melissa, Harold, and their sons arrived with furniture in a rental trailer, your client told them that it wasn't "convenient" to have Sam and Brett move in that day. This refusal to allow my clients to utilize the home as cotenants constitutes an ouster. Accordingly, your client owes rent to my clients for thirteen months (September, YR-01 through September, YR-00). Because the fair rental value of the home is $3,000 per month, the current amount due from your client is $26,000. I agree that my clients are responsible for their pro rata share of mortgage, insurance, and tax payments. These payments total $1,133.33 per month, or $13,600 for the past twelve months; their share of this sum is $9,067. Subtracting this sum from the rent your client owes, the net amount owed to my clients is $16,933. Note that under Madison law cotenants out of possession are not responsible for repair costs. Is your client in a position to pay this amount?

Very truly yours,

Greta B. Winston
Greta B. Winston

Honoring our nation's heroes

October 23, YR-00

Greta B. Winston
Attorney at Law
Muir & Winston
802 Market Street
Esperanza, Madison 55607

Dear Ms. Winston:

I regret to tell you that Madison National Bank has begun foreclosure proceedings on the Furmani family home. My client apparently received the enclosed notice of default in early September, but I have just learned about this situation. It appears that the Bank is unaware that Elbert Furmani is dead, since the notice was intended for him. This unfortunate situation is a direct result of the failure of your clients to meet their financial obligations.

Based on the information received from my client, it is clear that no "ouster" occurred. As your September 18 letter concedes, all that my client said was that it was not "convenient" for the boys to move in on the particular day they arrived. The clear implication of this language is that they *would* have been allowed to move in on a later day, one which was in fact convenient. But they made no effort to do so. Under these circumstances, your clients were not denied the right to enter and use the home. Thus, your clients are responsible for paying their respective shares of the mortgage, insurance, and tax payments, as outlined in my August 10 letter. The same is true for the repair costs, which were absolutely necessary to protect the home from inundation.

I again call on your clients to pay the amounts they owe. Otherwise, the home will be lost by foreclosure and all of our clients will suffer the consequences. As a sign of good faith, my client has agreed to remove his belongings from the small cottage in the rear of the property so that it can be rented out to a tenant and generate income to offset the carrying costs of the property.

Sincerely,

Kathleen B. Lawrence

Kathleen B. Lawrence
Attorney

TO: ELBERT R. FURMANI

NOTICE OF DEFAULT AND

ELECTION TO SELL UNDER MORTGAGE WITH POWER OF SALE

IMPORTANT NOTICE

NOTICE IS HEREBY GIVEN that Madison National Bank, the mortgagee under the mortgage executed by Elbert R. Furmani, mortgagor, dated March 15, 1988, and recorded on March 17, 1988, in Book No. 102, at Page 44, of the Official Records of Lancaster County, Madison, hereby declares that a breach of the obligation secured by the said mortgage has occurred, and that the nature of the breach is the failure to pay the monthly payment of $671 that was due on September 1, YR-00, and that the mortgagee hereby (1) declares that all sums secured by the said mortgage are immediately due and payable and (2) elects to sell or cause to be sold the mortgaged property to satisfy the obligation. The said mortgage encumbers that certain real property commonly known as 1032 Springdale Road, Esperanza, Lancaster County, Madison.

NOTICE IS FURTHER GIVEN that you have the legal right to bring your account into good standing and avoid foreclosure by paying all of your past due payments plus permitted expenses and costs within five business days prior to the date set for the sale of your property.

Dated: September 5, YR-00

Madison National Bank

Jackie Sue Shih
By: Jackie Sue Shih
Its: Vice President

MUIR & WINSTON
ATTORNEYS AT LAW
802 MARKET STREET
ESPERANZA, MADISON 55607
(792) 890-0337

November 1, YR-00

Kathleen B. Lawrence, Esq.
Madison Veterans Legal Center
1276 East Lincoln Blvd., Suite 19
Capital City, Madison 55481

Dear Ms. Lawrence:

My clients were shocked to learn that Robert had allowed the house to go into foreclosure. Please be advised that they recently reinstated the loan by paying the sum of $3,639 to Madison National Bank. This sum consists of (a) three monthly payments, each in the amount of $671, and (b) $1,626 in expenses incurred by the Bank during the foreclosure process. As a result, there is now no risk that the house will be lost by foreclosure. My clients will, of course, expect Robert to reimburse them for one-third of this payment.

As sympathetic as my clients are to Robert's personal and financial situation, it is clear that the current situation cannot continue. They cannot afford to allow Robert to live rent-free by himself in a five-bedroom house, while they bear most of the expenses. We have tried patiently to negotiate a resolution of this problem that would be satisfactory to both sides, but without success. Accordingly, my clients have decided to seek partition. Because there is no way to partition the property in kind, it must be partitioned by sale. This will allow Robert to use his share of the net sales proceeds as he wishes.

Under Madison law, a court will automatically grant partition when it is sought by any cotenant. As shown by the enclosed appraisal, the property is worth about $370,000. To avoid the expense of unnecessary litigation, my clients ask that Robert voluntarily agree as follows: (a) Melissa will list the property for sale with a real estate broker, with an asking price of $380,000; (b) the loan will be repaid from the sales escrow so that the buyer obtains title free and clear of the mortgage; (c) all siblings will cooperate in consummating the sale with the successful buyer, including by signing the deed; and (d) each sibling will receive one-third of the net sales proceeds. Please tell me as soon as possible whether this arrangement is acceptable to your client.

Very truly yours,

Greta B. Winston
Greta B. Winston

Tamara F. Moss, SRA
33 West Road
Esperanza, Madison 55607
(792) 782-9023

October 28, YR-00

Greta B. Winston, Esq.
Muir & Winston
802 Market Street
Esperanza, Madison 55607

Re: Appraisal of Furmani home

Dear Ms. Winston:

At your request, I have appraised the property located at 1032 Springdale Road, Esperanza, Madison ("Property") which is owned by members of the Furmani family. The Property consists of a detached single-family home (3,205 square feet) and a back yard cottage (918 square feet) which are located on a 1.7 acre lot, as shown on Exhibit A. The cottage is a self-contained living unit, which has been rented to tenants on occasion in the past.

I conclude that the fair market value of the Property as of the date of this letter is: $370,000. The basis for this opinion is as follows. Within the last three months, single-family homes in the Esperanza market have been selling for an average price of $88.57 per square foot. Since the two residences contain 4,123 square feet in total, this equates to a starting point of $365,174.

Because the two residences are 5.6 years older than the median home in the Esperanza region, a deduction of $10,000 from this starting point would be appropriate. However, the size of the parcel is somewhat larger than the median parcel size, which justifies a value increase of $23,000. The greater difficulty is adjusting the per square foot analysis for the fact that there are two residences on the parcel, rather than one larger residence. All the comparable sales during the study period have involved a single residence on a lot. On balance, I believe that a slight deduction would be appropriate because most home buyers do not wish to have a separate residence in the back yard. I estimate that this deduction would be about $8,000. These adjustments result in a value of $370,174, rounded to $370,000.

Sincerely,

Tamara F. Moss
Tamara F. Moss

Exhibit A
1032 Springdale Road, Esperanza, Madison
(not to scale)

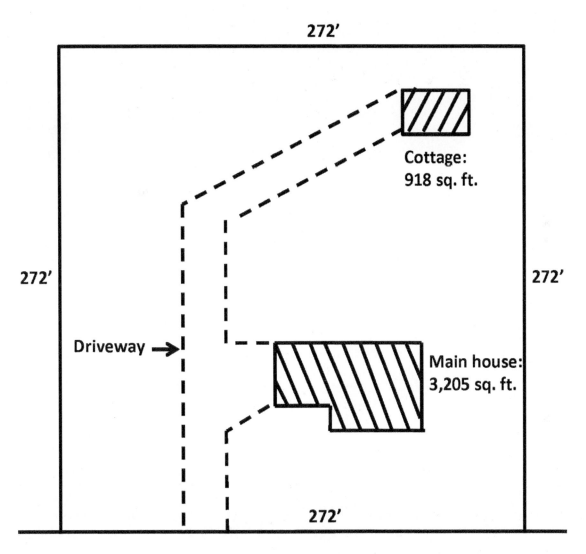

272'

272'

272'

Cottage:
918 sq. ft.

Driveway →

Main house:
3,205 sq. ft.

272'

Springdale Road

CHAPTER 5

MARITAL PROPERTY

A. INTRODUCTION

The exercise in this chapter involves marital property law. Today most states use the *modern common law system* for allocating rights in marital property (sometimes called the *separate property system*), while other states use the *community property system*. Madison uses the modern common law system.

This is a negotiation exercise that arises out of a divorce. You will act as an attorney for either the wife or the husband in attempting to reach an agreement on how the marital property should be divided.

The first part of the chapter provides an overview of the modern common law approach to marital property. It is followed by a section that gives you two new techniques to use in the negotiation. The final section is the case file of documents relevant to the dispute.

B. OVERVIEW OF THE LAW

The historic common law approach to marital property reflected profound gender bias in favor of the husband. During the 1800s, however, most states adopted the Married Women's Property Acts, which expanded the wife's property rights. These acts form the foundation of the modern common law approach to marital property.

1. *Rights during marriage:* The basic principle underlying the modern common law system is that during the marriage each spouse owns the property that he or she acquires. Thus, if W earns $50,000 in wages from working outside the home in a particular year, she owns that $50,000 and all assets purchased with this money. W has the exclusive right to manage and dispose of this property. Similarly, if H obtains $75,000 in royalties during the same year from his work as an author, he owns that money and all assets purchased with it.

2. *Rights during divorce:* The separate property principle of the modern common law system logically suggests that at divorce, each spouse should keep the property which he or she owns, without any sharing. However, this is not the majority view. As a matter of fairness, most states have modified the common law approach. Today most states require *equitable distribution* of the marital property, regardless of who originally acquired the property. This requires a judge to divide the marital property between the spouses in a just manner, considering a variety of factors which are typically set forth by statute. As a general matter, the judge has broad discretion in applying the equitable distribution factors.

Some states presume that an equal distribution is appropriate, absent special concerns, while others leave the distribution entirely to the discretion of the judge. Accordingly, depending on the law and the facts, if W and H have $1,000,000 in marital property when they divorce, it is possible that the judge might divide this sum equally, give $750,000 to W and $250,000 to H, or order a different distribution.

3. *Defining marital property:* Because "marital property" is distributed at divorce, it is vital to understand how such property is defined. In most states, the property subject to equitable distribution is defined as all earnings of either spouse during the marriage and all assets purchased with those earnings. In contrast, property which one spouse acquired before the marriage is not considered to be marital property.

4. *The "degree dilemma"—majority view:* Suppose that one spouse obtains a graduate degree during the marriage. If the couple later divorces, is the degree marital property which is subject to equitable distribution? Because the degree was acquired during the marriage, an argument can be made that it is "marital" property—if it is a type of property at all. However, the majority view is that a degree is *not* "property" and, accordingly, is not subject to equitable distribution. One of the most frequently-cited cases on this point is *In re Marriage of Graham*, 574 P.2d 75 (Colo. 1978), where the Colorado Supreme Court explained in detail why an M.B.A. degree was not a form of property.

5. *The "degree dilemma"—minority view:* Critics argue that the majority approach to the degree dilemma is both inequitable and poorly-reasoned. Most commonly, the issue arises when one spouse finances the other spouse's education, only to have the degree-recipient spouse file for divorce. In this situation, the couple has little or no marital property to divide. The biggest asset they have is the enhanced lifetime earning capacity of the spouse with the degree. Critics argue that it is unfair to ignore this reality, especially because the majority view seems to encourage divorce. More fundamentally, critics ask why the copyright to a novel or other literary work created during the marriage is considered to be marital property, while a degree is not. Both are intellectual achievements; both are intangible; and both have the potential to generate an income stream in the future.

C. NEGOTIATION TECHNIQUES

You learned these techniques in earlier chapters:

1. *Develop a plan for the negotiation.*

2. *Set appropriate goals for the negotiation.*

3. *Envision the negotiation from the other side's perspective.*

4. *Develop two goals: an aspirational goal and a bottom-line goal.*

5. *Ask questions.*

6. *Revisit the plan.*

This section will introduce you to two additional techniques:

7. *Keep in mind your BATNA—the best alternative to a negotiated agreement:* In any negotiation, each party has alternatives to reaching an agreement. For example, if A is negotiating to purchase land from B to build an apartment complex as an investment, A has many alternatives. Among other options, A could purchase land from another seller to build the complex, buy an existing apartment complex, or opt for a different type of investment altogether. Under the circumstances, usually there is one particular option which is better than the others. A good negotiator always keeps the BATNA in mind, because this drives his conduct during the negotiation. If the BATNA is better than the most favorable terms which he can negotiate, it makes sense to select the BATNA. Conversely, if the BATNA is less favorable than the most favorable terms which he can negotiate, it makes sense to take the deal.

8. *Be willing to walk away:* New negotiators often feel strong internal pressure to reach some sort of agreement, even if it is less favorable than the outcome the client should reasonably expect. This problem is particularly acute when the competing negotiator takes an unreasonable position and refuses any further compromise. Under these circumstances, it may be appropriate to end the negotiation—at least for the present. This places the competing negotiator in the potentially awkward position of having to explain to his client why his approach was unsuccessful. Of course, nothing prevents the parties from resuming negotiations at a later time on a more equal footing.

D. THE MEEHAN DIVORCE

Roy Meehan seeks a divorce from his wife, Darla Meehan, after a marriage which has lasted six years. During the marriage, Darla worked full time to support Roy while he attended law school and obtained a J.D. degree. Madison law allows for divorce without any showing of cause. Because the couple had no children, the only issue is how their marital property will be distributed. You will be an attorney representing either Roy or Darla in a negotiation to divide the property.

The case file below includes a copy of Madison Family Code § 805, which sets forth the test for allocating marital property upon divorce. The Madison Legislature based this section, in part, on the Principles of the Law of Family Dissolution that were adopted by the American Law Institute in 2000. Madison courts have not yet determined whether a degree is marital property.

Read the case file below as the first step in preparing for the negotiation. Your professor will provide you with confidential information concerning your side of the negotiation. As you work on your negotiation plan: (1) consider how the provisions of § 805 apply to the marital property owned by the Meehans; and (2) evaluate how likely it is that the Madison Supreme Court would rule that a degree is marital property.

Seabridge & Associates

Divorce Is All We Do
181 Ash Drive, Suite 200
Larchmont, Madison 55409
(790) 181-2209

September 3, YR-00

Mrs. Darla R. Meehan
37 Palawan Court
Larchmont, Madison 55410

Dear Mrs. Meehan:

As you presumably know, I have been retained by your husband, Roy D. Meehan, to institute a dissolution proceeding that will terminate your marriage. Madison law provides that either spouse may obtain a divorce decree without cause and regardless of fault. Because you and your husband have no children, the only issue which might be contentious in a dissolution proceeding is the distribution of the marital property.

Mr. Meehan and I hope that this proceeding can be as amicable and businesslike as is possible under the circumstances. Accordingly, we would like to work out an agreement for the division of the marital property before initiating the proceeding. This will allow the divorce to be finalized quickly, without the expense and delay of more litigation.

As I understand the situation, the marital property which you and your husband own is as follows: (a) a single-family home with a fair market value of $210,000, encumbered by a mortgage which secures repayment of a loan with a principal balance of $190,012; (b) a Jeep with a fair market value of $2,520; (c) a savings account with a balance of $15,102; (d) shares of stock in Apple with a fair market value of $30,889; and (d) furniture and other household items with minor value, probably about $5,000. Because a broker's commission of about $12,600 would be paid incident to the sale of the home, the net value of these assets is $60,899.

Madison law generally provides that the marital property is to be divided equally, unless certain special circumstances apply, as set forth in Madison Family Code § 805; I enclose a copy of this statute for your review. Mr. Meehan has no interest in claiming the benefit of any special circumstances at this time and is willing to divide the marital property equally, so that each of you receives approximately $30,450. Please consult with your attorney and inform me as soon as possible whether this proposal is acceptable to you.

Sincerely,

Dirk Seabridge
Dirk L. Seabridge

Madison Family Code § 805: Division of Marital Property

(a) Except as provided in subsection (b), all marital property shall be divided at dissolution so that each spouse receives an equal share.

(b) The spouses will be allocated unequal shares of the marital property only if one or more of the following subparts are applicable:

(1) If one spouse, without the other spouse's consent, made substantial gifts of marital property to third parties, or expended or destroyed marital property, the court shall increase the other spouse's share of the remaining marital property to compensate for such loss.

(2) If one spouse has lost earning capacity during the marriage due to his or her disproportionate share of the care of the marital children or the care of another sick, disabled, or elderly family member, the court shall increase that spouse's share of the remaining marital property to compensate for such loss.

(3) If one spouse gave up educational or occupational opportunities during the marriage which would have enhanced his or her earning capacity, or suffers from any disability or impairment which significantly limits his or her earning capacity, the court shall increase that spouse's share of the remaining marital property to compensate for such loss.

(4) If one spouse has significantly less wealth than the other spouse, the court shall increase that spouse's share of the remaining marital property to compensate for a portion of the loss in the standard of living which he or she would otherwise have experienced if the marriage had continued.

Family Law Group

A Professional Corporation
82 Spruce Avenue
Larchmont, Madison 55410
790.226.9081

September 29, YR-00

Dirk L. Seabridge, Esq.
Seabridge & Associates
181 Ash Drive, Suite 200
Larchmont, Madison 55409

Dear Mr. Seabridge:

Darla R. Meehan has asked me to represent her in connection with the dissolution proceeding which you mention in your September 3 letter. We agree that it would make sense to work out a mutually-agreeable property settlement, if possible. We also agree with the valuations which you have placed on the items of marital property which are listed in your letter.

Unfortunately, the offer contained in your letter overlooks the following facts:

(1) During the marriage, her husband Roy spent approximately $8,205 in marital assets purchasing lottery tickets over Darla's objections, but received only $3,110 in winnings, for a net loss of $5,095. Half of this, or $2,548, should be credited to Darla under Madison Family Code § 805(b)(1).

(2) Darla lost earning capacity during the marriage because she was required to care for her ailing mother on a substantially full-time basis for the last year and, as a result, her state certification as a dental technician lapsed. It will take her three months to obtain recertification, during which time she will lose approximately $7,250, representing 25% of a normal year's salary of $29,000. This amount should be credited to Darla under § 805(b)(2).

(3) You presumably know that Roy inherited approximately $450,000 from his great aunt this year, so he has substantial personal assets other than his share of the marital property. The value of Darla's personal assets, in contrast, is less than $1,000. Under these circumstances, it would be appropriate to credit Darla with $45,000 from the marital assets to compensate for the loss in her standard of living pursuant to § 805(b)(4).

Assuming that Darla receives the $54,798 in credits identified above, then the value of the marital property that you have identified so far would be allocated as follows: $60,899 less $54,798 equals $6,101 or $3,051 per spouse. Thus, Darla would receive a total of $57,849, and your client would receive $3,051.

However, your letter overlooks the most important item of marital property: the J.D. degree which Roy obtained in June, YR-01. You may be familiar with the Georgetown University study which shows that a J.D. graduate will earn $1,764,000 more over his lifetime than a person with a B.A. Of course, much of this value stems from work, not merely from holding the J.D. degree, so it would be inappropriate for Darla to receive half of this value, which would be $882,000. On the allocation question, we propose the following. Assuming that Roy has a 30-year career as an attorney, then the three years he spent in law school are roughly 10% of his total time in the legal profession. It makes sense that Darla should share in about 10% of Roy's total earnings increase, which would result in a payment to her of $88,200.

We concede that Madison courts have not yet determined whether a graduate degree is marital property. However, given the high quality of judicial decision-making in our state, I believe that there is a substantial possibility that our state supreme court would so hold if litigation ensued in this case, particularly given the short duration of this marriage (YR-05 to YR-00). Darla feels strongly that her economic and emotional support were vital in allowing Roy to obtain his degree. Roy was close to dropping out on two occasions, but Darla was able to convince him to continue. In addition, Roy was frequently rude and brusque with Darla, presumably due to the stress of law school, but she persevered because she knew that both she and Roy were investing in a law degree that would reward both of them in time. In addition, Darla worked full-time as a dental technician and her income was used to finance the couple's living expenses and Roy's tuition and books for all three years of law school (YR-04 to YR-01). Frankly, Darla finds it incredible that Roy wants to dissolve the marriage now, only a year after he obtained his J.D. degree. As the New Jersey Supreme Court stated in *Mahoney v. Mahoney*, 453 A.2d 527 (N.J. 1982), "*[m]arriage should not be a free ticket to professional education....*" (emphasis in original). For these reasons, Darla is prepared to take this issue to the Madison Supreme Court if necessary. In the interest of compromise, however, we will assume that she has only a 50% chance of prevailing on this point. Accordingly, she will accept a payment of $44,100 on this issue.

In summary, Darla is willing to accept a division of marital property by which Roy pays her the sum of $101,949 ($57,849 plus $44,100). Please inform me at your earliest convenience whether this offer is acceptable to your client.

Very truly yours,

Amy Y. Friedmann
Amy Y. Friedmann
Attorney at Law

Seabridge & Associates

Divorce Is All We Do
181 Ash Drive, Suite 200
Larchmont, Madison 55409
(790) 181-2209

October 15, YR-00

Amy Y. Friedmann
Family Law Group
82 Spruce Avenue
Larchmont, Madison 55410

Re: <u>Meehan v. Meehan</u>

Dear Ms. Friedmann:

I have now had the opportunity to consult with Mr. Meehan concerning the contents of your September 29 letter. I continue to hope that we can reach a mutually-satisfactory agreement on dividing the marital property.

I will first address the claim that Mr. Meehan's J.D. degree should be viewed as marital property. You are undoubtedly aware that virtually every state supreme court which has considered the issue has held that a graduate degree is not marital property. The leading decision is *In re Marriage of Graham*, 574 P.2d 75 (Colo. 1978), where the Colorado Supreme Court reasoned that a graduate degree was not property at all, but rather "an intellectual achievement that may potentially assist in the future acquisition of property." Thus, it is highly unlikely that the Madison Supreme Court would decide otherwise. It is telling that you cite *Mahoney v. Mahoney*, 453 A.2d 527 (N.J. 1982) in support of your position, because even that court refused to recognize a professional degree as marital property. It is, at best, speculation to assert that our state supreme court would deviate from the national consensus on this issue.

Moreover, the figures you cite concerning the economic value of a J.D. degree are substantially overstated, at least in the case of Mr. Meehan, because his plan is to help the poor by working as a legal aid attorney. He is currently employed by the Madison Legal Aid Society and earning a salary of only $38,500 per year, far below the amount that new associates are paid in large law firms. However, solely for the sake of facilitating a comprehensive agreement between the parties, and because of the love and affection which he still holds toward Mrs. Meehan, Mr. Meehan will agree to pay $5,000 to resolve this issue.

Turning to the other credits which you claim:

> (1) <u>Lottery tickets</u>: Millions of people buy lottery tickets, and some win. If Mr. Meehan had earned net winnings from his tickets, Mrs. Meehan would have shared in those benefits because they would be marital property. Since she would share any benefits, she

should also share any losses. In fact, § 805(b)(1) does not relate to this situation at all. It relates to situations where one spouse affirmatively destroys marital property, such as by intentionally chopping up a valuable painting. Accordingly, Mrs. Meehan is not entitled to any credit.

(2) <u>Care for mother</u>: It is true that Mrs. Meehan voluntarily gave up her job as a dental technician about a year ago and that she spent most of that year with her mother, Nina L. Van Etten. However, Mrs. Van Etten is only 54 years of age and, accordingly, is not "elderly" within the meaning of § 805(b)(2). Moreover, Mrs. Van Etten did not require a level of "care" which would require Mrs. Meehan to attend her on a full-time basis. Mrs. Van Etten was and is fully functional, except that she is confined to a wheelchair. Accordingly, Mrs. Meehan is not entitled to any credit. Indeed, if Mrs. Meehan persists in this claim, my client has instructed me to claim $14,500 from her as a credit, because she effectively destroyed marital property by not earning a salary for that year.

(3) <u>Mr. Meehan's inheritance</u>: It is well-settled in Madison that assets which one spouse acquires through devise or bequest are not considered as marital property and are not subject to distribution upon dissolution. Mrs. Meehan's claim under § 805(b)(4) appears to be an attempt to overcome this traditional rule by obtaining indirectly what the law says she cannot obtain directly. I do not believe that a court would allow such a claim. Moreover, that subsection applies only when it is necessary to compensate the spouse for a loss in the standard of living which she otherwise would have expected if the marriage had continued. In fact, Mr. Meehan never utilized any portion of his inheritance to increase the couple's standard of living, so Mrs. Meehan has lost nothing.

In conclusion, Mr. Meehan will agree to a division of the marital property under which he receives $25,450 and Mrs. Meehan receives $35,450. We feel that this allocation is fair. In addition, we believe that both parties would benefit from reaching a property settlement. This will allow a short dissolution proceeding, so that they can each proceed with their separate lives as soon as possible with minimal emotional turmoil. Please respond to this proposal at your earliest convenience.

Sincerely,

Dirk Seabridge

Dirk L. Seabridge

Family Law Group

A Professional Corporation
82 Spruce Avenue
Larchmont, Madison 55410
790.226.9081

October 22, YR-00

Dirk L. Seabridge, Esq.
Seabridge & Associates
181 Ash Drive, Suite 200
Larchmont, Madison 55409

Dear Mr. Seabridge:

Thank you for your recent letter in this matter. While the gap between the positions of our clients is wide, I share your hope that an agreement can be reached.
I have not previously raised the issue of fault. Technically, of course, fault is irrelevant under Madison law in the distribution of marital property. Yet, in equity, I believe that any judge would be troubled by your client's conduct, which suggests that he married Darla in bad faith. Under these circumstances, Darla believes that she is entitled to a share in the value of your client's degree. In the interest of compromise, Darla is willing to reduce her claim on this issue by half, to $22,050.

With regard to your positions on the credit issues:

(1) Any reasonable person knows that buying lottery tickets is a waste of money. The odds of winning the lottery are smaller than the odds of being struck by lightning.

(2) Mrs. Van Etten required care because she was confined to a wheelchair and, accordingly, was unable to perform such simple tasks as getting dishes from the cupboard or checking the mail box.

(3) As to your client's wealth, § 805(b)(4) makes no distinctions between earned wealth and inherited wealth, and none are warranted.

In summary, Darla will accept a division of the property by which Roy pays her the sum of $79,899 ($57,849 plus $22,050). Please respond as soon as possible.

Very truly yours,

Amy Y. Friedmann
Amy Y. Friedmann
Attorney at Law

CHAPTER 6

LANDLORD-TENANT LAW

A. INTRODUCTION

Since the 1960s, American landlord-tenant law has gone through revolutionary change. Traditionally, this law was oriented toward protecting the rights of landlords. But in recent decades, courts have greatly expanded the rights of residential tenants, often by using contract law principles to redefine the landlord-tenant relationship.

Perhaps the single most important innovation is the widespread adoption of the implied warranty of habitability: the residential landlord impliedly covenants that his leased premises are fit for human habitation. If the landlord breaches this obligation, the tenant is entitled to withhold rent until the problem is remedied. In addition, the tenant may assert this breach as a defense if the landlord brings an eviction action.

The exercise in this chapter is a short jury trial. The landlord brings an action to evict the tenant for nonpayment of rent; the tenant raises the defense that the landlord breached the implied warranty of habitability. You will act as the attorney for the landlord, as the attorney for the tenant, or as a witness in the trial. Depending on how your professor structures the exercise, you may also have the opportunity to act as a juror.

This chapter first provides an overview of the implied warranty of habitability. The next section discusses the procedural steps in a jury trial. The final section is the case file of documents for the exercise.

B. OVERVIEW OF THE LAW

The implied warranty of habitability was a response to a stark reality: many poor urban tenants were living in abysmal conditions. Disease, overcrowding, vermin, and filth threatened their health and safety. Many urban landlords found that they could maximize profits by spending little or no money on repairs and maintenance. In theory, local housing codes required that each dwelling unit meet certain minimum standards, but these codes were weakly enforced in many jurisdictions.

The District of Columbia Circuit adopted the implied warranty of habitability in the landmark case of *Javins v. First National Realty Corp.*, 428 F.2d 1071 (D.C. Cir. 1970), and it quickly spread to other jurisdictions, either by judicial action or by legislation. The *Javins* court held that a residential landlord was obligated to keep his premises in habitable condition. Because the tenant's duty to pay rent was dependent on the landlord's duty to maintain the premises, the court reasoned that the landlord's breach of the warranty allowed the tenant to withhold rent and raise the breach as a defense to an eviction action.

Four aspects of the implied warranty of habitability merit more detailed discussion:

1. *Standard for determining breach:* The most difficult issue is determining which conditions breach the warranty. It is widely agreed that major problems such as flooding, lack of electricity, or a leaky roof are normally significant enough to be violations. On the other hand, trivial and insubstantial defects such as torn wallpaper or peeling paint are not violations; the warranty does not require the landlord to maintain the premises in perfect condition. Between these extremes is a middle ground where the parameters of the warranty are less clear. The *Javins* court held that the scope of the warranty was defined by the District of Columbia's housing code; accordingly, a significant violation of the code was a breach of the warranty. Many courts follow this approach. However, most states have adopted a different standard, which broadly requires that the premises be fit for human habitation or words to this effect. For example, in *Hilder v. St. Peter*, 478 A.2d 202 (Vt. 1984), the Vermont Supreme Court held that the landlord must "deliver over and maintain, throughout the period of the tenancy, premises that are safe, clean and fit for human habitation." *Id.* at 208. Madison law follows the majority approach: the landlord must ensure that the premises are "fit for human habitation."

2. *Defects landlord is responsible for:* You may recall that under the constructive eviction doctrine the landlord is responsible for the acts or omissions of third parties only if she has the right to control those parties. In contrast, under the implied warranty the landlord is responsible for defects caused by any source except those that are caused by the tenant or the tenant's guests.

3. *Procedure for using the warranty:* In most states, the tenant must notify the landlord about the defects and allow a reasonable time for the landlord to make repairs before withholding rent. But the tenant is not required to vacate the premises.

4. *Measure of damages for breach:* If litigation occurs, it must be determined how much rent, if any, the tenant owes during the period when the defect existed. There is a split of authority on the measure of damages for breach of the warranty. Madison has adopted the percentage diminution approach. Under this method, the court determines the percentage by which the breach has reduced the tenant's use and enjoyment of the premises. Suppose T rents a house from L for $800 per month, but the roof leaks badly during any rainstorm. If the court finds that the defect reduced T's use and enjoyment by 75%, then T owes only $200 per month until the defect is fixed.

C. *WILLIAMS INVESTMENT CORPORATION v. LEWIS*

In this case, Williams Investment Corporation ("Williams") leased an apartment unit to the Lewis family ("Lewis"). Subsequently, Lewis withheld rent, claiming that Williams breached the implied warranty of habitability. Williams then filed an unlawful detainer action to evict Lewis and collect back rent. As its defense, Lewis asserts that Williams breached the implied warranty. The case file below contains the documents relevant to the case, including the pleadings filed by the parties, the jury instructions, and the verdict form.

Most states use expedited procedures for eviction lawsuits. Typically, no discovery is permitted, and the trials tend to be quite short.

The material in this section will introduce you to the steps in a simple jury trial. In order to give you the experience of participating in a complete trial, the exercise below has been streamlined so that it can be completed in approximately one hour. Your professor may give you additional instructions about the mechanics of the trial and/or modify the instructions below.

1. *Teams for trial:* This is a team exercise based on the documents in the case file below. In each trial, one team will represent Williams and the other will represent Lewis. There are two witnesses: (a) Morgan Estes, the manager of the apartment complex owned by Williams; and (b) Cary Lewis, one of the tenants. One member of each team will be its witness, and the others will act as attorneys. Each team will decide who will be its witness and who will have which attorney role.

2. *Attorneys:* Each attorney should prepare his or her opening/closing statements and witness questions in advance and in writing. If you are doing a direct examination, you will want to run through it with your witness *in advance.* All attorneys should come to the exercise dressed in professional, lawyer-like attire. Each attorney should stand up when addressing the judge, a witness, or the jury, and should call the judge "Your honor." Any objections should be short and to the point. The judge may ask opposing counsel to respond to an objection.

3. *Witnesses:* There is a witness statement in the file for each witness. Both witnesses are gender-neutral, so the roles can be played by students of any gender. Each witness is bound by his/her witness statement and may not testify in a manner that contradicts that statement. Witnesses may come to the exercise in attire which is consistent with their roles. The judge will administer this oath to each witness before he/she testifies: "Do you promise that the testimony you are about to give will faithfully and truthfully conform to the rules of the exercise?"

4. *Jurors:* The oldest member of the jury will serve as the foreperson, chairing the deliberations and filling out the verdict form. The youngest member of the jury will serve as the official timekeeper for the trial. If one of the attorneys exceeds his or her time, the timekeeper will politely

but firmly announce "Time," at which point the attorney must stop talking and sit down. The judge will enforce the time limits as necessary.

5. *Judge:* The judge will swear in the witnesses, rule on objections, give the jury its instructions, and otherwise supervise the trial. Only three types of objections are permitted:

(a) *"Objection. Calls for speculation."* A witness may only testify about his/her personal knowledge, and cannot guess or speculate;

(b) *"Objection. Irrelevant."* Only relevant evidence is allowed, meaning evidence which tends to make the existence of any fact that is of consequence to the determination of the action more probable or less probable than it would be without the evidence; and

(c) *"Objection. Leading."* A leading question is not allowed on direct examination, but is fine on cross-examination.

6. *Overview of trial:* The trial will proceed in the following sequence, with the indicated time limits. The steps are:

(a) statement of appearances by attorneys (1 minute);

(b) opening statement for plaintiff (3 minutes);

(c) opening statement for defendants (3 minutes);

(d) direct examination of Estes (8 minutes);

(e) cross-examination of Estes (6 minutes);

(f) direct examination of Lewis (8 minutes);

(g) cross-examination of Lewis (6 minutes);

(h) closing statement for plaintiff (3 minutes);

(i) closing statement for defendants (3 minutes);

(j) judge reads instructions to jury (4 minutes);

(k) jury deliberates (10 minutes); and

(l) jury foreperson reads verdict (1 minute).

7. *Statement of appearances:* The judge will call the case for trial, saying something like this: "I now call the case of Williams Investment Corporation v. Lewis. Are the attorneys present?" A Williams attorney will then say something like: "Your honor, I am _____ and I represent the plaintiff, Williams Investment Corporation, together with my co-counsel _____." A Lewis attorney will then make a parallel statement for the Lewis side. The judge will then say something like: "Counsel for plaintiff, you may proceed with your opening statement."

8. *Opening statement:* In the opening statement, each side explains to the jury what the evidence in the case will show. Do not include any argument in your opening statement; that belongs in your closing statement. In preparing the opening statement, you should carefully consider how the facts of the case do or do not fit into the instructions that the jury will receive from the judge. The parties agree on many of the facts, as you

can tell by comparing the complaint and the answer. The only issue in dispute at this point is whether Williams breached the implied warranty of habitability. If the warranty was breached, then Lewis cannot be evicted, and the jury should decide how much back rent, if any, Lewis should pay. If the warranty was not breached, then Lewis can be evicted and will owe all unpaid rent due under the lease.

9. *Direct examination:* After the opening statements are finished, the judge will turn to plaintiff's counsel and say something like: "Counsel, you may call your first witness." The attorney will then say: "Your honor, I call Morgan Estes." Estes will come forward, be sworn in by the judge, and sit in the witness chair. The same pattern will be followed for the defense witness, Cary Lewis. Direct examination is the opportunity for each side to develop its case by asking "direct questions" of its witness that will result in admissible evidence. Questions asked on direct examination are typically short and to the point, and do not "coach" or lead the witness about what the answer should be. For example, the Williams attorney might ask Estes: "Do any nearby apartment complexes have security bars on the windows?" This is a proper question on direct examination. But an attorney cannot ask a leading question during direct examination. A leading question is one that suggests the answer, like this: "Isn't it true that less than a third of the nearby apartment complexes have security bars on the windows?"

10. *Cross-examination:* When the direct examination of Estes is over, the judge will turn to defendants' counsel and say something like: "Counsel, you may cross-examine." The same pattern will be followed for the defense witness. This is the opportunity for each side to ask questions of the opposing party, based on his/her witness statement and the exhibits in evidence. Here, leading questions are both permitted and desirable. For example, the Williams attorney might ask Lewis: "Isn't it true that you never complained about any security problems until the afternoon of June 27?" One goal of cross-examination is to cast doubt on the testimony that the witness gave on direct examination. For example, you might try to show that the witness: (a) is mistaken; (b) has forgotten a fact; or (c) was not well-situated to make an observation. Or you might use cross-examination to force the witness to admit facts that hurt his or her case. But it is unwise to ask the witness to simply repeat what he/she said during direct examination.

11. *Closing statements:* When the cross-examination of Lewis is over, the judge will turn to plaintiff's counsel and say something like: "Counsel, you may proceed with your closing statement." This is the place for argument, as long as it is done in a professional manner. In the closing statement, each side explains to the jury why it should win the case, based on the evidence which was presented at trial. Here, you will be arguing about whether the evidence shows that the implied warranty of habitability was breached and, if so, how much rent Lewis should pay, if any. Each attorney should prepare his/her closing statement in advance, but should modify it as appropriate depending on what the evidence shows.

12. *Final steps:* Once the closing statements are over, the judge will read the jury instructions to the jury, which will then withdraw to another location to deliberate. During the deliberations, the attorneys and witnesses should remain in the courtroom area. Once the jury has reached a verdict, the judge will reconvene the trial, the jury foreperson will read the verdict, and the judge will then terminate the trial.

OLIVIA B. ERLICH
ERLICH & NELSON
102 Mountain Street
Oakdale, Madison 55402
(793) 556-0937

Attorneys for Plaintiff
WILLIAMS INVESTMENT
CORPORATION

SUPERIOR COURT OF MADISON

COUNTY OF JEFFERSON

WILLIAMS INVESTMENT
CORPORATION, a
Colorado corporation,

        Plaintiff,   No. 14-0672

vs.   COMPLAINT IN
                                 UNLAWFUL DETAINER

CARY LEWIS and
J.B. LEWIS,

        Defendants.

Plaintiff alleges:

1. Plaintiff WILLIAMS INVESTMENT CORPORATION is, and at all times mentioned herein was, a corporation organized and existing under the laws of Colorado with its principal place of business in Denver, Colorado. Plaintiff is, and at all times mentioned herein was, the owner of Apartment 108, 542 Central Avenue, Oakdale, Jefferson County, Madison (the "Apartment").

2. Defendants CARY LEWIS and J.B. LEWIS ("Defendants") are, and at all times herein mentioned were, residents of Jefferson County, Madison.

3. On August 30, YR-02, Plaintiff and Defendants entered into a written lease ("Lease") whereby Plaintiff leased the Apartment to Defendants on a month-to-month basis, and

Defendants agreed to pay Plaintiff $600.00 per month in rent, due on the first day of each month. A true and correct copy of the Lease is attached hereto as Exhibit 1.

4. Defendants entered into possession of the Apartment and paid the monthly rent pursuant to the terms of the Lease through June 30, YR-00. Defendants continue to occupy the Apartment.

5. Defendants failed and refused to make the monthly rental payment which was due pursuant to the Lease on July 1, YR-00. The sum of $600.00, which represents the unpaid rent, is now due and payable to Plaintiff.

6. Plaintiff has performed all terms and conditions of the Lease.

7. On July 10, YR-00, Morgan Estes, as an agent for Plaintiff, personally handed to Defendants a 3-day notice ("Notice") to pay rent or quit. The Notice included an election of forfeiture. A true and correct copy of the Notice is attached hereto as Exhibit 2.

8. The period specified in the Notice expired at the end of the day on July 13, YR-00, but Defendants have not paid the rent which is due and have not vacated the Apartment. Plaintiff is entitled to immediate possession of the Apartment.

9. At the time the Notice was served, the amount of rent due from Defendants was $600.00. The fair rental value of the Apartment is $20.00 per day.

WHEREFORE, Plaintiff prays for judgment as follows:

1. For immediate possession of the Apartment;

2. For past due rent of $600.00;

3. For damages at the rate of $20.00 per day from August 1, YR-00 for each day that Defendants remain in possession through entry of judgment;

4. For costs of suit incurred herein;

5. For such other and further relief as the Court may deem proper.

Dated: July 15, YR-00
ERLICH & NELSON

By: *Olivia B. Erlich*
Olivia B. Erlich

LEASE

This Lease is entered into on   August 30, YR-02   by and between Williams Investment Corporation ("Landlord") and   Cary Lewis and J.B. Lewis   ("Tenant"). Landlord and Tenant hereby agree as follows:

1. Basic Provisions: Landlord rents to Tenant, and Tenant rents from Landlord, the real property commonly described as   Apartment 108, 542 Central Avenue, Oakdale, Madison   ("Premises"). The term of this Lease will begin on   October 1, YR-02   and will continue as a month-to-month tenancy thereafter. Either Tenant or Landlord may terminate the tenancy by giving written notice to the other at least 30 days before the intended termination date.

2. Rent: Tenant agrees to pay the sum of $600   per month in rent to Landlord during the term of this Lease. Rent shall be paid on the first day of each month.

3. Occupants: The Premises may be occupied by no more than   two (2) persons.

4. Pets: Pets shall not be allowed on the Premises without the prior written consent of Landlord.

5. Condition of Premises: Tenant agrees to keep the Premises clean and sanitary, to properly dispose of all wastes, and to otherwise use the premises in an appropriate manner.

6. Assignment and Sublease: Tenant shall not assign this Lease, nor shall Tenant sublease all or any portion of the Premises, without the prior written consent of Landlord.

7. Default: If Tenant should fail to pay rent when due or fail to perform any other term of this Lease, after not less than 3 days written notice of such default is given to Tenant in the manner required by law, Landlord may elect to terminate all rights of Tenant hereunder.

8. Attorney's Fees: If legal action is brought to evict Tenant or to otherwise enforce the terms of this Lease, the court may award attorney's fees to the prevailing party.

Morgan Estes, agent for Williams Investment Corp.
Landlord

Cary Lewis J.B. Lewis
Tenant(s)

EXHIBIT 1

NOTICE TO PAY RENT OR QUIT

To: Cary Lewis and J.B. Lewis

Within 3 days of service of this notice, you are required to pay the rent now due and unpaid on the premises at   Apartment 108, 542 Central Avenue, Oakdale, Madison   in the amount of $ 600, representing rent due for the month of   July, YR-00 or to deliver possession of the premises to the undersigned.

Your failure to pay the amount demanded or to deliver possession of the premises within 3 days will cause the undersigned to initiate legal proceedings against you to declare a forfeiture of your lease, to recover possession of the premises, and to recover the rent due through the expiration date of this notice and damages for each day of occupancy thereafter, plus attorneys fees.

You are further notified that the undersigned elects to declare the forfeiture of the lease under which you hold possession of the premises, if you fail to pay the amount of rent demanded above.

Morgan Estes, as agent for
Williams Investment Corp.
Landlord

July 10, YR-00
Date

EXHIBIT 2

NORMAN J. BALDWIN
BALDWIN & ASSOCIATES
334 Forest Road
Oakdale, Madison 55402
(793) 667-9055

Attorney for Defendants
CARY LEWIS and J.B. LEWIS

SUPERIOR COURT OF MADISON

COUNTY OF JEFFERSON

WILLIAMS INVESTMENT
CORPORATION, a
Colorado corporation,

        Plaintiff,   No. 14-0672

vs.   ANSWER

CARY LEWIS and
J.B. LEWIS,

        Defendants.

Defendants CARY LEWIS and J.B. LEWIS ("Defendants") answer the complaint in this action by admitting, denying, and alleging as follows:

1. Answering the allegations set forth in Paragraphs 1, 2, 3, 4, and 7, Defendants admit the same.

2. Answering the allegations set forth in Paragraph 5, Defendants admit that they did not make a monthly rental payment for July, YR-00. Defendants deny the remaining allegations set forth in said paragraph.

3. Defendants deny the allegations set forth in Paragraphs 6 and 9.

4. Answering the allegations set forth in Paragraph 8, Defendants admit the same, except that Defendants deny that any rent is due or that Plaintiff is entitled to possession of the Apartment.

AS AND FOR AN ADDITIONAL DEFENSE TO PLAINTIFF'S COMPLAINT, DEFENDANTS ALLEGE AS FOLLOWS:

AFFIRMATIVE DEFENSE

Plaintiff breached the implied warranty of habitability by failing to install a deadbolt lock and security bars at the Apartment and by failing to install adequate lighting in the common area of the apartment complex.

WHEREFORE, Defendants pray for judgment as follows:

1. That Plaintiff take nothing by its complaint herein;

2. That Plaintiff be ordered to (a) make repairs and correct the conditions that constitute a breach of the implied warranty of habitability and (b) reduce the monthly rent to zero until the conditions are corrected;

3. For costs of suit incurred herein;

4. For such other and further relief as the Court may deem proper.

Dated: July 24, YR-00   BALDWIN & ASSOCIATES

By: *Norman J. Baldwin*

Norman J. Baldwin

Witness Statement of Morgan Estes

I am 32 years old. I actually have two jobs. I work 25 hours per week as a reporter for the Oakdale Herald, and I also am the manager of the Oakdale Ranch Apartments which takes about 10-15 hours a week; I live in apartment 101. The apartment building, which consists of 28 units (14 on the first floor, and 14 on the second) was built in 1957. It is owned by Williams Investment Corporation, which is based in Denver. The company owns a lot of apartments, all over the U.S.

The building is in the shape of a "U", with a small pool area in the middle of the U, and a parking lot surrounding the U. All the units are accessed by exterior corridors; and the second floor is reached by going up an exterior staircase. There are three lights down by the pool which we keep on at night. Otherwise, all the night lighting in the complex comes from light shining through the windows of the apartments.

I rented apartment 108 to Cary and J.B. Lewis in YR-02. The lease they signed is Exhibit 1 to the complaint in this action. Before they signed the lease, Cary did ask about whether the neighborhood was safe, and I said it was. This was true; we had never had any serious crime problems during the four years I had managed the building.

Apartment 108 is a ground floor unit, with two windows looking out into the central courtyard. Neither those windows nor any other windows in the complex have security bars. In fact, I recently checked all of the apartments within a three-block radius; of the 22 apartment buildings in this region, only nine have security bars on the windows. And those security bars can also be dangerous; there is supposed to be a special latch to let the occupant out if there's an emergency, like a fire, but if that latch doesn't work, the tenant would be locked in.

Neither apartment 108 nor any other unit in the complex has a deadbolt lock, except for mine. I installed the deadbolt lock with my own money early this year, but only because I often receive rent payments in cash, so I sometimes have as much as $4,000 or $5,000 in cash in the apartment overnight until I can take it to the bank. As a matter of company policy, Williams has instructed all apartment managers that we are not authorized to use company funds to install deadbolt locks on unit doors or other safety features unless the tenants are in clear and immediate danger. The reason for this is that if we have to spend money for deadbolts, more lighting, and so forth, we will have to raise the rents to pay for the costs. I have not checked to see how many buildings in the area have deadbolts on the apartment doors, but I am sure that some of them do. I agree that a deadbolt lock does provide more safety for a tenant, at least in some situations; but they are not really needed in our building.

It is true that there was a burglary in apartment 105 in September, YR-01. But I'm not sure that a deadbolt lock would have made any difference; the burglar might have still pushed in the door. Realize that the doors in the complex aren't made of steel; they're just wood.

The incident in apartment 103 on June 23 last summer was not actually a burglary at all. It was more of a domestic dispute. The couple who lived there had gotten into an argument; she locked him out; he returned in the middle of the night and forced his way in through the door to recover what he thought was his property. When she screamed, he grabbed a few items and fled.

Finally, the June 26 burglary in apartment 208 was quite real—and scary. But how can anyone stop something like that? We would have to convert the apartment complex into a prison camp, with barbed wire and guard dogs. And even if there had been a deadbolt, it would have made no difference, because they got in through a window.

I wrote an article about local crime for the Herald back in April of this year. There were 27 residential burglaries within six blocks of the complex in a three month period. But this averages only nine burglaries per month, spread out over perhaps 500 apartment units. And those kids who hang out across the street that the Lewises are worried about? They're just teenagers hanging out, doing what teenagers do. They are not criminals. Remember that I also live in the complex, and I have always felt safe.

I did receive a letter from Cary on June 27, at about 4:00 p.m. S/he demanded that the company pay to install a deadbolt lock, window bars, and new lighting. Even if the company felt these changes were necessary, they couldn't be made in a day or two. It would take weeks, probably months, to do all these things, though I guess if it was just a deadbolt this wouldn't take too long, maybe a day or two.

When I became the manager, I bought a Taser with my own funds because I knew I would be collecting cash rents sometimes. When I saw how worried the Lewises were, I offered to let them have my Taser for a while, to give them a sense of security. But they refused it, rather rudely as I recall.

I handed the Lewises a Notice To Pay Rent or Quit on July 10, but they never paid any more rent. The notice is Exhibit 2 to the Complaint in this case.

Dated: September 5, YR-00   *Morgan Estes*

Witness Statement of Cary Lewis

I am 69 years old. I live with "J.B.", my husband/wife, at the Oakdale Ranch Apartments, 542 Central Avenue in Oakdale, apartment number 108. I am now retired, but during my working years I was a letter carrier for the postal service, while J.B. taught math at Oakdale Junior High. We have lived in Oakdale for 32 years.

We used to live in a nice single-family home in Oakdale Heights for many years, but we lost it in foreclosure a few years ago. We had refinanced the loan, but when the adjustable interest rate kicked in, our monthly payments doubled, and we couldn't afford to keep the house. In the process, we lost most of our savings for retirement. So when the house went, we needed to find a cheaper place to live.

In August, YR-02, I saw an ad in the Oakdale Herald for the Oakdale Ranch Apartments, and J.B. and I visited to check the place out. Before we got there, we knew it was in a rundown part of town, but they were offering 2-bedroom units for only $600 per month. It was a two-story, 28-unit apartment building owned by Williams Investment Corporation, and the resident manager was Morgan Estes. The building wasn't fancy, but it wasn't bad either; and the neighborhood seemed OK. Morgan showed us several units, but we liked 108 the best because it was on the ground floor, so we did not have to climb any stairs. Before we signed anything, I asked Morgan how safe the neighborhood was. S/he replied: "It's very safe. We've never had any problems." We then signed a written month-to-month lease for the unit, for $600 per month. My attorney has a copy of the lease.

J.B. and I moved into the apartment in October, YR-02, and everything was fine for the first year or so. But in September, YR-01, there was a burglary in one of the ground floor units, number 105, just about 50 feet away from us. The burglars just forced the door open around 3:00 a.m., ran in to grab the computer, TV, and other electronic equipment, and fled before anyone could react; fortunately, the tenants were away at the time. There is no lighting in the parking lot or exterior hallways of the apartment building, so the burglars had no trouble getting in and out. Also, the door to unit 105 did not have a deadbolt lock, which is why the burglars could pry it open.

I really hadn't thought about all this before, but I realized that our apartment might also be unsafe as well, given the lack of outdoor lights and the fact that our door didn't have a deadbolt lock either; our door lock was just one of those little buttons you push in the handle. But a deadbolt gives you 2 or 3 inches of steel that goes into the 2 by 4s surrounding the door; there's no way to knock down a door with good hinges on one side and a good deadbolt on the other side. And there weren't any security bars on our windows either, which some other apartment complexes in the area did have. It was just about then, maybe November, YR-01, when we started seeing groups of kids, teenagers, hanging out at the vacant lot across the street. They were there at all hours, maybe doing drugs, we could never be sure. But it sure made us feel uneasy, coming home sometimes late with all that darkness outside around the building.

Last spring, the Herald published an article about a crime wave that was spreading through our part of town. In the first three months of the year, there were 27 residential burglaries within six blocks of our apartment. This article made all of us nervous, so I again asked Morgan whether s/he really thought we were safe; I think this was in May. S/he told me that the owner, the investment company, cared about the safety of tenants, and wanted to make sure we were safe, or something like that. S/he also told me that the only crime which had ever occurred at the building was that burglary in number 105, which s/he said was "an isolated incident."

But things got worse this last summer. On June 23, someone broke into apartment number 103 using a crowbar; he just pried the door open in the middle of the night. But the tenant was there and screamed, so the burglar got scared I guess and ran away. And then on June 26, someone smashed one of the large windows in unit 208, upstairs, again at night, held the tenants at gunpoint and ransacked the apartment, taking jewelry and cash. All this made J.B. and me so upset that we couldn't even sleep for the rest of that night.

On June 27, J.B. and I spent hours discussing what to do. It was too expensive to move, but we felt completely unsafe, and it seemed like the owner and Morgan were not taking our concerns seriously. We decided to write them a letter, demanding that they fix things: install a deadbolt lock on our apartment door, security bars on our windows, and much better lighting in the apartment's parking lot and exterior hallways. A copy of that letter is Exhibit A to my statement. That afternoon I handed the letter to Morgan in a sealed envelope. S/he said s/he would read it, but I don't know if s/he ever did.

The rent was due on July 1. But J.B. and I didn't pay it because Morgan and the company had not done anything at all to fix the problem. When Morgan dropped by that afternoon to ask where the rent check was, I said we weren't going to pay it and explained why. Morgan said that my June 27 letter didn't give her/him enough time to fix the problems, and s/he offered to give me a "Taser" so that I could zap any burglars who tried to get in. But I said: "How can I zap them if they come in while I'm asleep? Or what if they have guns?" Morgan didn't have an answer for this. And I can't believe that she/he didn't have enough time to deal with the problems. S/he knew all about the burglaries, the kids across the street, and so forth. And Morgan could have gotten a locksmith out here to install a deadbolt lock, at least, in less than a day. I spent some time walking through apartment complexes in our neighborhood yesterday, and I saw that a lot of units, maybe most of them, did have deadbolt locks

On July 10, Morgan handed J.B. and me a piece of paper with the title "Notice to Pay Rent or Quit." We didn't pay it. Six or seven days later, someone came to the front door (which still does not have a deadlock, by the way) and handed us a summons and complaint.

Dated: September 8, YR-00   *Cary Lewis*

86

The Lewis Family
542 Central Avenue, Apartment 108
Oakdale, Madison 55402

June 27, YR-00

Morgan Estes, Manager
Williams Investment Corporation
542 Central Avenue
Oakdale, Madison

BY HAND DELIVERY

Dear Morgan:

Given all the crime that is going on in our part of Oakdale, we no longer feel safe in our apartment. As you know, there have been a number of break-ins in our complex, and that article you wrote for the Herald showed that there is a real crime wave in the area. The unsafe conditions in our apartment violate the implied warranty of habitability.

We hereby request that your company do the following as soon as possible: (1) install a deadbolt lock on our apartment door; (2) install security bars on our apartment windows; and (3) install much better lighting in the parking lot and the exterior hallways.

If your company does not take these basic steps to protect our safety, we will have no choice but to exercise our rights under the implied warranty and withhold rent until these things are done.

Sincerely,

Cary Lewis   *J.B. Lewis*
Cary Lewis   J.B. Lewis

EXHIBIT A

SUPERIOR COURT OF MADISON

COUNTY OF JEFFERSON

WILLIAMS INVESTMENT
CORPORATION, a
Colorado corporation,

      Plaintiff,

vs.   No. 14-0672

CARY LEWIS and
J.B. LEWIS,
      Defendants.

JURY INSTRUCTIONS

1. This is an action for what is called unlawful detainer. Plaintiff Williams Investment Corporation, the landlord, claims that defendants Cary Lewis and J.B. Lewis, the tenants, failed to pay rent and no longer have the right to occupy the leased property. Plaintiff seeks to recover possession of the property and back rent. The defendants agree that they did not pay rent, but they raise a special defense: that they still have the right to occupy the property because the plaintiff did not maintain it in habitable condition.

2. You must decide whether the plaintiff did maintain the property in habitable condition. In order to win on this defense, the defendants must prove three things:

    a.   The plaintiff failed to ensure that the premises were fit for human habitation;

    b.   The defendants did not substantially contribute to the creation of the claimed habitability problem; and

    c.   The defendants notified the plaintiff about the claimed habitability problem and gave the plaintiff a reasonable amount of time to fix it before withholding rent.

3. In deciding whether the property was fit for human habitation, you should remember that a property is still habitable even if it has a few minor defects. However, a property is not fit

for human habitation if it contains a problem that has a material impact on the health or safety of the tenant. The fact that the defendants have continued to occupy the property does not necessarily mean that the property is habitable.

4. If you find that the defendants have established all three elements set forth in Paragraph 2 above, then you should find that defendants are entitled to remain in possession of the property. In this event, you must decide the amount of back rent that the defendants owe to plaintiff, if any, given the habitability problem. To do this, you must determine the percentage by which the uninhabitable condition reduced the defendants' use and enjoyment of the premises, and then apply that percentage to the amount of back rent that would otherwise be due to the plaintiff. The parties agree that if the premises were fully habitable the rental value would be $600.00 per month. Accordingly, you must determine what percentage of that amount per month, if any, the defendants should pay to the plaintiff.

5. If you find that the defendants have failed to establish one or more of the three elements set forth in Paragraph 2 above, then you should find that plaintiff is entitled to possession of the property and unpaid rent in the amount of $600.00 per month.

6. You should now retire to the jury room to decide upon your verdict. I have given the foreperson the form of verdict which you should use. The foreperson will notify me when your verdict is ready.

Superior Court Judge

SUPERIOR COURT OF MADISON

COUNTY OF JEFFERSON

WILLIAMS INVESTMENT
CORPORATION, a
Colorado corporation,

        Plaintiff,

vs.   No. 14-0672

CARY LEWIS and
J.B. LEWIS,

        Defendants.

VERDICT

We, the jury in this action, hereby render our verdict as follows:

_____   We find for the plaintiff. Plaintiff is entitled to possession of the property, and defendants shall pay the sum of _____to plaintiff.

_____   We find for the defendants. The defendants are entitled to possession of the property. The uninhabitable condition(s) reduced defendants' use and enjoyment of the property by ____%, so defendants shall pay the sum of _____ to plaintiff.

CHAPTER 7

REAL PROPERTY SALES

A. INTRODUCTION

Under the common law doctrine of *caveat emptor*, the seller of real property generally had no obligation to disclose defects to the buyer. But over the last 50 years, most states have adopted the rule that the seller of residential real property, such as a single-family house or condominium unit, has a duty to disclose known defects under some circumstances.

The exercise in this chapter is a short jury trial. The buyers of a home bring an action seeking damages for the seller's alleged failure to disclose certain problems. You will act as the attorney for the buyers, the attorney for the seller, or a witness in the trial. Depending on how your professor structures the exercise, you may also have the opportunity to act as a juror.

This chapter first gives you an overview of the law governing the seller's duty to disclose. The next section is a summary of the procedural steps in the trial, following the pattern used for the trial in Chapter 6. The final section is the case file of documents for the exercise.

B. OVERVIEW OF THE LAW

Traditionally, the seller of real property had no duty to disclose defects unless she: (1) affirmatively misrepresented the condition of the property to the buyer; (2) actively concealed its defects; or (3) owed a fiduciary duty to the buyer. Accordingly, in most instances the buyer had complete responsibility to assess the condition of the property.

Today, in most jurisdictions, the seller of residential real property has a broad duty to disclose known defects to the buyer. Although the precise phrasing of the rule varies from state to state, in general the seller is obligated to disclose defects he knows about that (1) materially affect the value or desirability of the property and (2) are not known to or reasonably discoverable by a buyer. *See, e.g., Johnson v. Davis*, 480 So. 2d 625 (Fla. 1985); *Lingsch v. Savage*, 29 Cal. Rptr. 201 (Ct. App. 1963).

Three aspects of the disclosure duty merit more detailed discussion:

1. *Material defects:* It is often difficult to determine whether a particular defect is so significant that it must be disclosed. It is widely accepted that major physical defects such as a leaky roof, substantial termite damage, or a defective heating system are sufficiently material to require disclosure. On the other hand, trivial and insubstantial defects need not be disclosed. The majority of states use an objective standard to determine materiality, though states differ on how this is done. One approach is to

measure materiality by diminution in market value; if a defect would significantly reduce the value of the property, then it must be disclosed. Another approach is to ask whether the defect would significantly affect the desirability of the property to a reasonable person. As you will see in the jury instructions, Madison follows the second approach.

2. *Defects not readily discoverable by buyer:* Obvious and apparent defects that a reasonably prudent buyer would notice during a visual inspection of the property—such as large foundation cracks or a collapsing ceiling—need not be disclosed. Beyond this point, however, there is uncertainty about the scope of the buyer's inspection duty. The phrasing of the "not reasonably discoverable" standard indicates that the buyer is only charged with knowledge of defects that could be "reasonably" obtained. At a minimum, any defect that could be discovered by an ordinary adult (without special knowledge or training) doing a visual inspection of the property need not be disclosed. In fact, virtually any defect could be discovered by a buyer who expends enough time and money to investigate the property. In the classic case of *Stambovsky v. Ackley*, 572 N.Y.S.2d 672 (App. Div. 1991), the court held that the seller was obligated to disclose that the house was allegedly haunted, in part, because "the most meticulous inspection and . . . search would not reveal the presence of poltergeists at the premises or unearth the property's ghoulish reputation in the community." *Id.* at 676. Although presumably the buyers could have discovered this simply by asking neighbors whether they knew of any problems with the house, the court apparently believed that this level of inspection went beyond what a buyer was reasonably required to do. It is not clear whether most other states would endorse this position. As the jury instructions reflect, Madison law requires the buyer to prove that she "could not have reasonably discovered" the defect.

3. *Remedies:* It is widely accepted that actionable nondisclosure justifies rescission of the sales agreement. Alternatively, the successful plaintiff may opt to receive compensatory damages. The most common measure of damages is based on how much the defect reduces the fair market value of the property. Madison follows this view, as the jury instructions indicate; damages are equal to the difference, if any, between (a) the purchase price the buyer paid for the property and (b) the fair market value at the time of the sale given the presence of the defect.

C. *POWELL v. KNOX*

In this case, Jamie Knox sold a single-family home to Jordan and Hunter Powell ("Powells"), a married couple. The Powells allege that they later discovered two problems with the home: (1) very noisy parties were sometimes held at a house across the street; and (2) vegetables could not be grown in the soil in the backyard of the home due to contamination. The Powells filed a lawsuit against Knox seeking damages for this alleged nondisclosure. The parties have agreed that the case will be handled under a special set of rules for streamlining the trial. The case file below contains all of the documents relevant to the case, including the pleadings, the jury instructions, and the verdict form.

This trial follows the same pattern as the trial in Chapter 6. In order to give you the experience of participating in a complete trial, the exercise has been simplified so that it can be completed in approximately one hour. Your professor may give you additional instructions about the mechanics of the trial and/or modify the instructions below.

1. *Teams for trial*: This is a team exercise based on the documents in the case file below. In each trial, one team will represent the Powells and the other will represent Knox. There are two witnesses: (a) Hunter Powell; and (b) Jamie Knox. One member of each team will be its witness, and the others will act as attorneys. Each team will decide who will be its witness and who will have which attorney role.

2. *Overview of trial:* The trial will proceed in the following sequence, with the indicated time limits. The steps are:

(a) statement of appearances by attorneys (1 minute);

(b) opening statement for plaintiffs (3 minutes);

(c) opening statement for defendant (3 minutes);

(d) direct examination of H. Powell (8 minutes);

(c) cross-examination of H. Powell (6 minutes);

(f) direct examination of Knox (8 minutes);

(g) cross-examination of Knox (6 minutes);

(h) closing statement for plaintiffs (3 minutes);

(i) closing statement for defendant (3 minutes);

(j) judge reads instructions to jury (4 minutes);

(k) jury deliberates (10 minutes); and

(l) jury foreperson reads verdict (1 minute).

3. *Additional information about the trial:* For additional information about (a) what the attorneys, witnesses, jurors, and judge will do during the trial and (b) the procedural steps in the trial, see the discussion in Chapter 6, Section C. The provisions set forth there also apply to this trial.

Manning, Zuber & Dunleavey
A Professional Corporation
52 Redbud Lane
Larchmont, Madison 55410
(790) 902-3311

October 15, YR-01

Mr. Jamie F. Knox
Larchmont Senior Residential Center
181 Spruce Avenue
Larchmont, Madison 55409

Re: <u>Powell v. Knox</u>

Dear Mr. Knox:

I have been retained as counsel for Jordan and Hunter Powell in connection with your failure to disclose certain serious problems with the house which you sold to them, located at 47 Country Club Circle in Larchmont.

I am enclosing a copy of the complaint against you which was filed today in Plata County Superior Court in order to save you the embarrassment of being served by a professional process server. Please consult an attorney as soon as possible to make sure that your rights are protected in this matter and show him or her the complaint. I am sure that your attorney will be willing to accept service of process on your behalf.

As your attorney will explain, the Powells have chosen to file this lawsuit under a special procedure which the Court has adopted in certain cases to save time and money for all parties, as described in detail on the attached document entitled "Expedited Procedure for Small Cases." You will note that this special procedure may only be used where the amount in controversy is $50,000 or less and certain other conditions are met. You must also agree to this procedure if it is to be used. Please consult with your attorney to determine if you are willing to give your consent to this procedure.

Very truly yours,

Scott T. Zuber

Scott T. Zuber

SUPERIOR COURT OF MADISON

COUNTY OF PLATA

EXPEDITED PROCEDURE FOR SMALL CASES

Pursuant to Madison Code of Civil Procedure § 225.6, the Superior Court for the County of Plata has been selected as one of five counties in the state to utilize an expedited procedure in certain civil cases as part of an experimental program. The goal of the program is to simplify and accelerate litigation, and thereby reduce expense and delay.

In order for this procedure to apply to a particular case, the following conditions must be met: (a) the case must be a civil case where the amount in controversy is $50,000 or less; and (b) all parties to the case must agree to the use of the procedure.

The following rules will apply in all cases tried under this expedited procedure:

(1) Each side may call only one witness.

(2) No expert witnesses may be used.

(3) No discovery is permitted, except that each side is required to provide each other side with a detailed statement of what its witness will say during the trial. The witness may not testify to matters which are not set forth in the statement.

(4) Attorneys may object to trial testimony only if a question: (a) calls for speculation; (b) asks about irrelevant material; or (c) is a leading question during direct examination.

(5) The trial must not take any longer than one hour.

(6) Either side may demand a jury trial.

Dated: January 1, YR-02

Wilma G. Rowlette
Presiding Judge

SCOTT T. ZUBER
MANNING, ZUBER & DUNLEAVEY
A Professional Corporation
52 Redbud Lane
Larchmont, Madison 55410
(790) 902-3311

Attorneys for Plaintiffs
JORDAN POWELL and HUNTER POWELL

SUPERIOR COURT OF MADISON

COUNTY OF PLATA

JORDAN POWELL and
HUNTER POWELL,

          Plaintiffs,   NO. 76-0087

vs.   COMPLAINT

JAMIE F. KNOX,

          Defendant.

Plaintiffs allege as follows:

1. At all times mentioned herein, plaintiffs JORDAN POWELL and HUNTER POWELL ("POWELLS") were individuals residing in Plata County, Madison, and were married to each other.

2. At all times mentioned herein, defendant JAMIE F. KNOX ("KNOX") was an individual residing in Plata County, Madison. Prior to April 23, YR-01, KNOX held fee simple absolute title to a single-family residence commonly known as 47 Country Club Circle, Larchmont, Plata County, Madison (the "Home").

3. On January 23, YR-01, the POWELLS entered into a written contract to purchase fee simple absolute title in the Home from KNOX. A true and correct copy of this contract is attached as Exhibit A and incorporated herein by reference as though set forth in full. Pursuant to this contract, escrow on the purchase transaction closed on April 23, YR-01, and the POWELLS became the owners of fee simple absolute title in the Home on that day. The

POWELLS have used the Home as their principal residence from April 23, YR-01 until the present.

4. Plaintiffs are informed and believe, and thereon allege, that KNOX was aware of the following facts concerning the Home on and before January 23, YR-01, and thereafter:

A. The Smith family which lives across the street from the Home regularly holds parties that produce extremely loud noise that renders the Home unsuitable as a residence; and

B. The soil in the backyard of the Home is contaminated with dangerous pesticides, such that it is unsuitable for growing any vegetables for human consumption.

5. Defendant KNOX failed to disclose these facts to the POWELLS before they acquired title to the Home. These facts were not known to the POWELLS, and the POWELLS could not reasonably have discovered them. Plaintiffs are informed and believe, and thereon allege, that KNOX knew that they did not know and could not reasonably have discovered these facts, and purposefully and intentionally failed to disclose them, in order to induce the POWELLS to purchase the Home. These facts significantly affect the value of the Home and the desirability of the Home to a reasonable person. Had the POWELLS been aware of these facts, they would not have consummated the sales transaction and obtained title to the Home.

6. Plaintiffs have been damaged as a result of the failure of KNOX to disclose the above facts in an amount which plaintiffs are informed and believe, and thereon allege, is approximately $50,000. Plaintiffs will seek leave of court to amend this complaint to set forth the exact amount of compensatory damages they have suffered when the same can be ascertained.

WHEREFORE, plaintiffs pray for judgment as follows:

1. For compensatory damages according to proof;

2. For costs of suit incurred herein; and

3. For such other and further relief as the Court may deem proper.

Dated: October 15, YR-01   MANNING, ZUBER & DUNLEAVEY

By: *Scott T. Zuber*
Scott T. Zuber

PURCHASE AND SALE AGREEMENT

This Purchase and Sale Agreement ("Agreement") is made on   January 23, YR-01 between   Jamie F. Knox   ("Seller") and   Jordan and Hunter Powell   ("Buyer").

1. Seller agrees to sell and Buyer agrees to buy that certain real property ("Property") commonly known as
          47 Country Club Circle, Larchmont, Madison
and described as follows
Lot 86 as shown on that certain subdivision map of "Country Club Estates" recorded in Book 207, Page 55, Official Records of Plata County, Madison, on November 18, 2001

2. The purchase price for the Property is $705,000   which shall be paid to Seller in cash at the close of escrow.   Within five (5) days after the execution of this Agreement by both Buyer and Seller, Buyer shall give seller a deposit in the amount of $70,000   which shall be applied to the purchase price at the close of escrow. Obtaining the loan(s) described below is a contingency of this Agreement: Not applicable.

3. This transaction will be consummated through an escrow established with Pioneer Escrow Company, 11 Green Plaza, Madison.   The closing date on the escrow will be   April 23, YR-01.   Seller will deliver possession of the Property to Buyer at close of escrow.

4. At close of escrow, Seller shall by general warranty deed convey to Buyer a fee simple absolute estate in the Property free and clear of any and all encumbrances, liens, mortgages, deeds of trust, and other title defects of any kind or nature, except for real property taxes which are not yet delinquent and the following:
Conditions, covenants, and restrictions as set forth in that certain "Declaration of Conditions, Covenants, and Restrictions for Country Club Estates," recorded in Book 212, Page 7, Official Records of Plata County, Madison, on January 13, 2003.

Buyer shall take title as follows: Jordan Powell and Hunter Powell, as joint tenants with right of survivorship

5. Real property taxes and assessments shall be prorated as of the close of escrow. Seller will pay the costs and expenses incurred in clearing title and preparing, executing, acknowledging, and delivering the deed. Buyer shall pay all recording fees. Buyer and Seller shall each pay one half of the escrow fee.

EXHIBIT A

6. The Property is sold in its present condition as of the date this Agreement is executed. Seller makes no representations or warranties about the condition of the Property. Buyer acknowledges that before close of escrow Buyer is free to conduct any and all inspections, investigations, tests or surveys of the Property that Buyer deems appropriate, either directly or through appropriate professionals, at Buyer's own expense. Buyer shall have the right, in Buyer's sole discretion, to cancel this Agreement until five (5) days before   April 23, YR-01 based on the results of said inspections, investigations, tests, or surveys.

7. As used herein, the Property includes all existing fixtures and fittings that are attached to the Property, together with all electrical, mechanical, lighting, plumbing and heating fixtures, built-in appliances, awnings, shutters, attached floor coverings, television antennas, satellite dishes, air conditioners, pool/spa equipment, mailbox, water softener, and security systems/alarms except for the following:
The dining room chandelier is not included in this sale and will be removed by Seller before close of escrow.

8. Buyer acknowledges that upon close of escrow, Seller has agreed to pay compensation to   Larchmont Properties, a licensed Madison real estate broker
for its services in this transaction. Buyer agrees and acknowledges that   Larchmont Properties is a real estate broker representing the Seller in this transaction. Seller agrees and acknowledges that   not applicable   is a real estate broker representing the Buyer in this transaction. Seller acknowledges that part of the compensation paid to   not applicable
may be shared with   not applicable.   A real estate broker is the person qualified to advise on real estate transactions. Buyer and Seller acknowledge and agree that if either of them desire legal or tax advice in connection with this transaction, an appropriate professional will be consulted.

9. Time is of the essence. The terms of the Agreement are intended by the parties as a final, complete, and exclusive expression of their Agreement with respect to the Property and this transaction, and may not be contradicted or modified by evidence of any prior agreement or contemporaneous agreement. Neither this Agreement nor any provision in it may be extended, modified, amended, or altered except in a writing executed by Buyer and Seller.

Executed on the day and year first written above:

Jamie F. Knox
Seller: Jamie F. Knox

Jordan Powell   Hunter Powell
Buyer: Jordan Powell, Hunter Powell

EXHIBIT A

ELEANOR C. MATTE-NORTH
MADISON SENIOR ADVOCATES, INC.
317 North Central Avenue, Suite 15G
Larchmont, Madison 55410
(790) 901-3305

Attorneys for Defendant
JAMIE F. KNOX

SUPERIOR COURT OF MADISON

COUNTY OF PLATA

JORDAN POWELL and
HUNTER POWELL,

        Plaintiffs,   NO. 76-0087

vs.   ANSWER

JAMIE F. KNOX,

        Defendant.

Defendant JAMIE F. KNOX appears herein and answers the Complaint as follows:

1. Defendant has no information or belief concerning the allegations set forth in Paragraph 1, and accordingly denies each and every such allegation.

2. Defendant admits the allegations set forth in Paragraphs 2 and 3.

3. Defendant denies each and every allegation set forth in Paragraphs 4, 5, and 6, except that defendant admits he never told plaintiffs about the supposed "facts" concerning party noise and soil contamination which are described in Subparagraphs A and B of Paragraph 4.

WHEREFORE, defendant prays for judgment as follows:

1. That plaintiffs take nothing by their complaint;

2. For costs of suit incurred herein; and

3. For such other and further relief as the Court may deem proper.

Dated: November 8, YR-01   MADISON SENIOR ADVOCATES, INC.

                             By: *Eleanor Matte-North*

                                 Eleanor C. Matte-North

Witness Statement of Jamie F. Knox

I am 89 years old. I worked as a bank manager for many years before retiring when I hit 60. After that, my spouse Riley and I bought 47 Country Club Circle in Larchmont, where we lived for many years. We were avid golfers, and some of the first buyers in the area. When we bought, it was affordable; but the house has increased in value so much over the years that I couldn't afford to buy it now. After Riley died, I realized that the house was just too big for one person—5 bedrooms, 4 bathrooms, and so forth, all on 2.6 acres. Also, I was lonely. So last year I decided to sell the place and use the money to move into the Larchmont Senior Residential Center. To get in, you have to pay $325,000, and then you pay about $7,000 per month while you're there. But you get everything—a small apartment, meals in the dining room, lifetime medical care, social activities.

I listed the house for sale with Frank Sherman over at Larchmont Properties in early January, YR-01. Frank had represented the seller in the deal when we bought the house, so he knew the house and he knew us. It made sense to go back to him. After I called him, Frank came over, looked the place over again, and told me he would figure out how much I should ask for. A few days later, he phoned me to say that it would probably go for about $730,000, maybe as high as $750,000. I decided to list the house for sale at $760,000 so that I would have room to negotiate; I figured that any potential buyer would offer less than that. We had it on the market for a few days when the Powells offered $705,000. It seemed very low to me at the time, but really I wanted to sell the house and move into the Center, so I decided to take it. But I do think it was worth more than that, probably at least $730,000 or $740,000. I signed a purchase and sale contract with the Powells, and the deal closed on April 23, YR-01. There was still a mortgage on the house and I had to pay the broker's commission, so I end up netting only about $343,000 from the sale. I used most of this to buy into the Center.

The contract said that the Powells could conduct any inspections of the property they wanted, as long as they paid for them. They could bring in experts, whatever they wanted. But they never did. The one time they came to see the place was around January 20 in YR-01. That time they didn't even go into the backyard. They walked up the front sidewalk, spent maybe 15 minutes rushing through the inside of the house, and then left. I don't know if they even looked out the window into the backyard. They certainly didn't seem to care about it. And they didn't ask me any questions about the house. Not one. If there was anything they wanted to know, they should have asked me. I would have told them whatever they wanted.

Now the Powells are suing me, and I don't know exactly why. They say that there are old pesticide residues in the backyard, which means they can't have a vegetable garden there because it would be dangerous to eat the food. I don't know anything about that. I'm not a pesticide expert. Before the land was developed for houses, I think it was used to grow corn. Maybe there was some sort of pesticide used on the corn that was allowed then, but which everyone knows is dangerous now. I just don't know. No one ever told me that there were any pesticides on my property. Personally, I don't believe in using them. Riley and I used to plant a beautiful flower garden in that backyard, and we always used organic gardening techniques.

The reason we never grew a vegetable garden is that they are too much work for what you get. I can buy vegetables at the store, any time. Riley and I liked flowers, so that's what we planted there. Now that I think about it, the neighbors around us never had vegetable gardens either. I guess that some people would find this to be a bit odd, never having any vegetable gardens around the neighborhood. I never thought about it at the time. I suppose I thought that everyone just liked flowers more.

I don't know why anyone thinks that not having a vegetable garden would reduce the value of the house. In my opinion as a former bank manager, it would have no impact on the value. Plenty of folks don't have those gardens. In fact, these days it's rare to see anyone anywhere with a vegetable garden, wherever you live. People eat fast food more. They want convenience. During World War II, then there were lots of vegetable gardens. We had to have them. But not now. I just can't believe that the Powells would really want a garden. Neither one said anything about gardening to me. In fact, I think they told me that they planned to spend most of their summers in Europe. But that's when you would garden, in the summer. I suppose if they really wanted to grow vegetables, they could grow them in pots or planters.

I know the Powells are also complaining about some parties that were held at the Smith house across the street. They say I should have warned them about the parties. Well, everyone has parties from time to time, don't they? Riley and I went to a few parties at the Smiths, years ago, and they were terrific! Anything you wanted to drink or eat—they had it. And it could get pretty wild, with the dancing and all, drunk people diving into the pool with their clothes on, 20 or 30 at the same time, acting like fools. The Powells say the Smiths are holding parties that are really loud. I wouldn't know about that. My hearing isn't very good, hasn't been for years. None of my neighbors ever complained about parties, as far as I know.

Sure, after Riley died, I sometimes saw cars parked across the street in the Smith's driveway and on the street, mainly on some Friday nights during the summer months. I assumed there was a party going on when that happened, but I never went over. The Smiths have a lovely backyard with a big patio and that pool, perfect for summer parties. But the cars never blocked traffic or anything like that. They didn't cause any problems that I knew about. There were a few times, maybe five or six times in the ten years the Smiths were there before I moved out, when I noticed a police car there on a Friday night. I didn't go out to investigate because it was late. The second Smith boy, Dillon, he's a troublemaker, always having some difficulty with the police. I thought the police were there about Dillon when I saw those cars.

Can't someone have parties without neighbors complaining? Parties are fun. Everyone has them. It's just part of living a good life. I can't believe that anyone could seriously argue that living across the street from a house where parties were held would be a problem or affect the value of property in any way. Maybe the Powells are just angry because the Smiths didn't invite them to the parties. Look, if the Powells were really worried about noise and it was as bad as they claim, they could have sued the Smiths to make them stop. You know, we all have to put up with occasional annoyances when we live in a neighborhood. It's part of life. Even if the noise was as bad as the Powells now claim, it wouldn't have any impact on the value of the house.

I have heard that the Powells are having financial problems now. Maybe that's why they're suing me. It was something about their investments going bad. And I heard that two or three of their creditors had put some liens on the house. Again, I don't know the details.

The Powells wrote me a letter last July asking to buy my chandelier. A copy of that letter is Exhibit 1 to this statement. The letter didn't mention anything about the Smiths' parties, so the Powells certainly weren't worried about the noise then. As you can see, they did raise a claim about pesticides, but it clearly didn't affect the value of the house because they offered to ignore it if I would sell them my chandelier. I wrote back in September, after I got out of the hospital; a copy of my letter is Exhibit 2. In that letter, I made it clear that I did nothing wrong when I sold the house.

Dated: January 20, YR-00   *Jamie F. Knox*
                                     Jamie F. Knox

July 22, YR-01

Jamie Knox
Larchmont Senior Residential Center
181 Spruce Avenue, Apt. 3K
Larchmont, Madison 55409

Dear Mr./Ms. Knox:

We are writing with regard to the large crystal chandelier that used to hang in the dining room. Of course, the agreement provided that you could remove it, as you did before we took occupancy. Yet it seemed to fit the room so well. We have been trying to find a replacement chandelier, but without success so far.

Would you be interested in selling the chandelier to us? While we are not certain whether you are currently in a situation where it is of use to you, it would certainly be of great use to us. It appears that new chandeliers of that type cost about $5,800 if they can be found at all. We would be willing to pay you the same price for your chandelier, even though it has been used. Please call us at your convenience to discuss this offer.

By the way, we were surprised to learn that there seems to have been some minor pesticide contamination in the backyard many years ago, which makes the soil unsuitable for growing vegetables. We are lucky that the Larchmont Farmers' Market is so close to our house, so that we can purchase organic produce easily. It seems to us that you should have told us about the contamination. But if you agree to sell us the chandelier on the above basis, we will be happy to let that pass and let bygones be bygones.

With best wishes,

Jordan Powell
Jordan Powell

Hunter Powell
Hunter Powell

EXHIBIT 1

Larchmont Senior Residential Center
181 Spruce Avenue
Larchmont, Madison 55409

Serving seniors is our business...and our pleasure!

September 4, YR-01

Powell Family
47 Country Club Circle
Larchmont, Madison 55409

Dear Powell Family:

Thanks for your recent letter. I'm sorry for the delay in responding, but I have had a bit of health trouble so I've been in the hospital.

No, I'm not interested in selling the chandelier. That's why I wanted to hold on to it when I sold the house. The chandelier has many special memories for me. It is somewhat big for my present living quarters, but I have gotten it installed and I appreciate it every day.

I was surprised to hear about any pesticide contamination. Certainly my spouse Riley and I never knew about anything like that. We grew beautiful flowers in the yard every year, so I really don't think there are any pesticides there. They would have stunted the flowers. I'm sure you didn't mean this, but I almost sense a threat of litigation in your letter. That would be unfortunate. There are too many lawsuits in this country already, and I did absolutely nothing wrong when I sold you the house.

Sincerely,

Jamie Knox
Jamie Knox

P.S. Have you been invited to any of the Smiths' parties yet? They were terrific!

EXHIBIT 2

Witness Statement of Hunter Powell

My spouse Jordan and I are the plaintiffs in this lawsuit. I am 38 years old, and my spouse is the same age. We are suing Jamie Knox because s/he did not disclose two serious defects in connection with the house we bought, 47 Country Club Circle, Larchmont, Madison. A true and correct copy of the Purchase and Sale Agreement for the house is attached to the Complaint in this action as Exhibit A. We entered into that Agreement on January 23, YR-01. Escrow on the purchase closed on April 23, YR-01, and we took possession of the house the same day.

After we were married, Jordan and I lived in our house in the Hamptons in New York for most of the year, but spent the summer in a small country house which we own in France, in the Loire Valley. Jordan had been trained as an architect, though s/he never ended up working in architecture. I was trained as a physician, but I never actually held a full time job as such. I did volunteer as a doctor from time to time during the year in a free clinic in the Hamptons, helping patients in need. Jordan's parents were well off; they were killed in a skydiving accident when Jordan was 22, and s/he inherited their family company which makes compact disks for music albums. The company is run by professional managers, so Jordan never had to work for a living, nor did I.

About two years ago, Jordan and I decided to make a major change in our lives by moving to Madison. It's a slower, friendlier lifestyle here, compared to the Hamptons. And Jordan was interested in using his/her architectural skills to create some kind of low-cost housing for the homeless in Capital City. As you know, that's a huge problem. Anyway, we are golfers, and Larchmont was located within commuting distance of Capital City, with a great golf course, so we decided to move to Larchmont.

When we flew out to Madison to look at homes over a weekend in January of last year, we saw a newspaper advertisement about 47 Country Club Circle in Larchmont. We called the broker, Frank Sherman, who arranged for us to tour it on a Tuesday afternoon. It was a good size for us: two stories, about 3,600 square feet, with lots of room to have dinner events and parties. It had plenty of bedrooms for overnight guests, on a good-sized lot, 2.6 acres, and it was close to the golf course. It was located on a nice street, with other large homes.

On the day we went through the house, there was an older person there; s/he didn't tell us who s/he was, but later we learned that it was the owner, Jamie Knox. I did have some questions about the house I would have asked if I had known s/he was the owner. As I remember it, we spent about 30 to 45 minutes checking out the house. We inspected every room; and we looked out every window, because views are important to us. Because we were pressed for time, we didn't actually walk out into the backyard. But we saw the yard while looking out the windows. About half of it was grass, and the other half was just soil. It looked like some sort of annual plants had been growing there during the season, maybe a vegetable garden or maybe flowers. Since it was January, though, it was too cold for any annual plants to be growing.

We didn't hire any contractors or other experts to check out the house. With hindsight, we certainly should have. The Agreement said we could. But we were still living in the

Hamptons, and it was just too hard to coordinate all that from New York. And we didn't have a broker in the deal. Again, maybe we should have had a broker who could look out for our interests. We trust people, and we assumed that Frank Sherman and Jamie Knox were honorable people, that they would tell us if there were any problems with the house.

After we moved into the house in April, the first big problem we noticed was the loud Friday night parties at the Smith house, just across the street at 46 Country Club Circle. Those parties started in late April and continued through the end of September, every week; there were 23 parties in total over the summer. The pattern was always the same. Cars started appearing around 8:30 or 9:00 p.m.; they filled the Smiths' large driveway and took up most of the vacant parking spaces on the block. There must have been 15 or 20 cars, each with two or three people in them. They all went into the Smith house, some of them carrying bottles of alcohol of some kind. By 9:30 or 10:00 p.m., the noise level in our house was very high, as loud say as a vacuum cleaner if your ear is two feet away from it. I think that's about 75 decibels. It was so loud that Jordan and I could not carry on a normal conversation. The first time this happened, I went over, knocked on the Smiths' door, and complained, but all they did was invite us to join the party. Then I called the police, who said that they had been out to the Smith house many times, always on a Friday night, because all the neighbors had complained about the noise. But the officer said there was nothing the police could do, because there is no ordinance in Larchmont which makes it a crime to emit loud noise. I don't know why not; we should have such an ordinance. Look, Jordan and I sometimes vacuum our own house, so we're used to that noise for very short periods. But not for hours at a time. This noise usually continued until about 2:00 a.m.; then Jordan and I were finally able to get to sleep. On party nights, Jordan and I ended up wearing earplugs after 10:00 p.m. to block out the noise, which was partially effective; it reduced the noise level to a dull roar. Of course, this meant we couldn't talk to each other. Jamie Knox must have known all about the noise; after all, s/he lived there for years and that letter s/he sent us shows that s/he attended some of those parties.

The other problem was the dangerous contamination in the backyard. In May, Jordan and I planted a vegetable garden in part of the backyard. It was about 100 feet deep and 200 feet wide, covering about a half acre. We planted seeds for corn, beets, carrots, lettuce, beans—all of our favorites. Ever since my days in medical school, I have believed that home-grown, organic produce is the best diet for humans. Accordingly, Jordan and I intended that our garden would be totally organic. So we were shocked in early June, when Lori Tesso, one of our neighbors to the north, told us that the whole area was contaminated with a pesticide and that any vegetables grown in our backyard would be dangerous for humans to eat. I called the Plata County Agricultural Extension Office, which confirmed that during the 1950s an experimental pesticide called "Frintal C" had been sprayed on corn in the area which included our property. It later turned out that Frintal C was proven to increase the risk of cancer in laboratory animals, so the U.S. Environmental Protection Agency eventually banned its use on food crops. The most recent research shows that eating even one serving of food grown in soil contaminated with Frintal C increases the risk of contracting liver cancer by 5%. That may not sound like much, but no one takes chances with cancer. Maybe I'm more concerned than some other people are, because of my training as a physician. I know that there is no "safe" level of exposure to cancer-causing substances. No one in our neighborhood grows vegetable gardens, so Jamie Knox must have known that there was a big problem with the soil. In fact, Lori told us that everyone in the whole neighborhood knew about this cancer danger. It is true that Jordan and I offered to overlook this problem if Mr./Ms. Knox would sell us the chandelier, but that happened before we went to a lawyer and learned about our rights.

Jordan and I would certainly not have bought the house if we had known about these problems. We paid $705,000 for the house, assuming that there were no problems. These problems clearly lower the value of the house. I'm not an appraiser, but I believe that the house was probably worth no more than $655,000 when we bought it, given these problems. When we sell the house, we will have to tell the buyers about the problems, and I'm certain this will reduce the sale price we can get.

Jordan will be unable to attend the trial in this case because s/he is involved in a Chapter 11 proceeding back in New York in connection with the family company. It has some financial problems right now because CD sales are slipping. But this is not the reason we are suing Mr./Ms. Knox. Our personal finances are in good shape. We're suing because we were defrauded.

Dated: January 22, YR-00

Hunter Powell
Hunter Powell

SUPERIOR COURT OF MADISON

COUNTY OF PLATA

JORDAN POWELL and
HUNTER POWELL,

          Plaintiffs,   NO. 76-0087

vs.   JURY INSTRUCTIONS

JAMIE F. KNOX,

          Defendant.

1. The plaintiffs in this action are Jordan Powell and Hunter Powell, who purchased a home from the defendant, Jamie F. Knox. Plaintiffs claim that the defendant is liable for damages due to his failure to disclose certain information about the home: (a) that neighbors across the street were holding extremely noisy parties; and (b) that vegetables could not be grown in the soil in the backyard of the home. The defendant agrees that he did not provide such information to the plaintiffs, but he denies that he is liable in this case.

2. In order to establish their claim concerning noise, the plaintiffs must prove all of the following:

(a) The neighbors across the street were holding extremely noisy parties;

(b) The defendant knew this information, but the plaintiffs did not know it and could not reasonably have discovered it;

(c) The defendant knew that the plaintiffs did not know and could not reasonably have discovered this information;

(d) The information significantly affected the desirability of the home to a reasonable person; and

(e) As a result, the plaintiffs were harmed.

If you find that the plaintiffs have proven all five elements in this paragraph, then you should find for the plaintiffs on this issue. If you find that the plaintiffs have failed to prove one or more of these elements, then you should find for the defendant on this issue.

3. In order to establish their claim concerning vegetables, the plaintiffs must prove all of the following:

(a) Vegetables could not be grown in the soil in the backyard of the home;

(b) The defendant knew this information, but the plaintiffs did not know it and could not reasonably have discovered it;

(c) The defendant knew that the plaintiffs did not know and could not reasonably have discovered this information;

(d) The information significantly affected the desirability of the home to a reasonable person; and

(e) As a result, plaintiffs were harmed.

If you find that the plaintiffs have proven all five elements in this paragraph, then you should find for the plaintiffs on this issue. If you find that the plaintiffs have failed to prove one or more of these elements, then you should find for the defendant on this issue.

4. If you find that the plaintiffs have proven either one or both of their claims against the defendant, then you must decide how much money will reasonably compensate the plaintiffs for the harm. This compensation is called "damages." The damages that the plaintiffs claim are the difference between (a) the purchase price they paid for the home, which was $705,000, and (b) the fair market value of the home at the time of the sale. If you find that the fair market value of the home was less than $705,000 at the time of the sale, then you should award the difference in value to the plaintiffs. If you find that the fair market value of the home was $705,000 or more at the time of the sale, then you should award nothing to the plaintiffs.

5. You should now retire to the jury room to decide upon your verdict. I have given the foreperson the form of verdict which you should use. The foreperson will notify me when the verdict is ready.

Superior Court Judge

SUPERIOR COURT OF MADISON

COUNTY OF PLATA

JORDAN POWELL and
HUNTER POWELL,

          Plaintiffs,   NO. 76-0087

vs.   VERDICT

JAMIE F. KNOX,

          Defendant.

        We, the jury in this action, render our verdict as follows:

_____ We find for the plaintiffs. Plaintiffs are entitled to compensatory damages in the amount of _____.

_____ We find for the defendant. Plaintiffs are not entitled to damages.

Dated: _____   Signature of foreperson: _____

CHAPTER 8

NUISANCE LAW

A. INTRODUCTION

The exercise in this chapter explores the private nuisance. At common law, the nuisance doctrine was the principal tool used to resolve land use conflicts. Today zoning laws and other land use regulations have partly supplanted the doctrine, but it remains important in some situations.

This is a negotiation exercise based on a dispute between neighboring landowners. One family has a solar energy system mounted on the roof of their house; the owner of the adjacent vacant lot plans to build a high house on its property, which will partially block sunshine from reaching the solar system. You will act as an attorney for one of the landowners in trying to negotiate a resolution of the dispute, using principles of nuisance law.

The first section of the chapter provides an overview of nuisance law. It is followed by a section that gives you two new techniques to use in the negotiation. The final section is the case file of documents relevant to the dispute.

B. OVERVIEW OF THE LAW

Restatement (Second) of Torts § 821D defines a *private nuisance* as "a nontrespassory invasion of another's interest in the private use and enjoyment of land." In contrast, a *public nuisance* is an improper interference with a right common to the public.

In order to prevail in a private nuisance case, the plaintiff must prove that the defendant's conduct resulted in an intentional, nontrespassory, unreasonable, and substantial interference with the use and enjoyment of the plaintiff's land. These elements are discussed in more detail below.

1. *Intentional:* The defendant's conduct is intentional if he acts for the purpose of causing the harm or he knows that harm is resulting or substantially certain to result from his conduct. For example, if O knows that his factory emits a nauseating odor which drifts onto P's land, but fails to prevent this from occurring, O's conduct is intentional.

2. *Nontrespassory:* The interference must not involve any physical entry onto the land of another. For example, noise, vibration, light, and odors are viewed as nontrespassory invasions. A physical entry onto the land of another is governed by the trespass doctrine.

3. *Unreasonable:* Jurisdictions differ about the meaning of this element. Some states cling to the traditional *gravity of the harm* test: the defendant's conduct is unreasonable if it causes substantial harm, regardless of the social utility of the conduct. Accordingly, if the odor from O's factory sometimes causes P's family to become sick, this element is probably met, regardless of the value of O's factory. Many states—including Madison—use the Restatement (Second) of Torts standard: the defendant's conduct is unreasonable if the *gravity of the harm* outweighs the *utility of the conduct.* In determining the gravity of the harm under the Restatement test, five factors are considered: (a) the extent of the harm involved; (b) the character of the harm involved; (c) the social value that the law attaches to the type of use or enjoyment invaded; (d) the suitability of the particular use or enjoyment invaded to the character of the locality; and (e) the burden on the person harmed of avoiding the harm. In determining the utility of the conduct under this test, three factors are considered: (a) the social value that the law attaches to the primary purpose of the conduct; (b) the suitability of the conduct to the character of the locality; and (c) the impracticability of preventing or avoiding the invasion. In the O-P example, a court using the Restatement test would weigh the harm caused by the odor (sickness suffered by P's family) against the utility of the factory (value of its products, jobs, etc.). Finally, a number of states use multi-factor tests that fall somewhere between these two approaches.

4. *Substantial interference:* There must be a "real and appreciable invasion of the plaintiff's interests." Restatement (Second) of Torts § 821F cmt. c. In other words, a minor or trivial impact on the plaintiff's interests is insufficient. In the O-P example above, the severity and frequency of illness caused by the odor probably meet this standard.

5. *Use and enjoyment of land:* The defendant's conduct must interfere with the use and enjoyment of land, e.g., by causing physical damage to the property or personal injury to occupants. In the O-P example, P is injured in his capacity as a landowner because his family members suffer sickness while living on the property.

In the typical nuisance case, the plaintiff sues for (1) an injunction requiring the defendant to end the nuisance and (2) damages caused while the nuisance existed. However, a plaintiff may also sue for an injunction in advance where the defendant intends to begin conduct that will constitute a nuisance.

C. NEGOTIATION TECHNIQUES

Remember the basic negotiation techniques you learned in prior chapters:

1. *Develop a plan for the negotiation.*

2. *Set appropriate goals for the negotiation.*

3. *Envision the negotiation from the other side's perspective.*

4. *Develop two goals: an aspirational goal and a bottom-line goal.*

5. *Ask questions.*

6. *Revisit the plan.*

7. *Keep in mind your BATNA.*

8. *Be willing to walk away.*

This section will introduce you to two additional techniques:

9. *Negotiate from interests, not positions.* Try to keep the negotiations focused on the interests of each side, rather than on the specific positions each is taking. In this context, an interest is a desire, concern, or other motivation. A position is the method the party has chosen to advance or protect its interests. Negotiating parties sometimes become locked into their competing positions and lose sight of what their interests are. A negotiation that directly deals with interests will usually be more productive than one that is centered on positions.

10. *Use legitimizing sources.* A legitimizing source is an objective criterion that supports your position in the negotiation. Use it in discussions with the other side. As a general rule, the more objective the source, the more valuable it will be. In legal negotiations, the most commonly-used legitimizing source is the law. For example, if it is 90% certain that the governing law favors one side, this will have a determinative impact on the negotiation. Other legitimizing sources include fair market value, professional opinions, standards adopted by professional organizations or government agencies, and the like.

D. THE SINCLAIRS' SOLAR ENERGY SYSTEM

The parties in this exercise are Verna and James Sinclair, who own a home with a rooftop solar system, and Quality Construction Company ("Quality"), which owns the vacant lot to the south of the Sinclair home. Quality plans to build a house on its lot with a very high roof; the shadow from this roof will interfere with the Sinclairs' system. The Sinclairs argue that the shadow caused by the planned house would be a nuisance. You will be an attorney representing either the Sinclairs or Quality in a negotiation to resolve the dispute.

This exercise is based on the facts of *Prah v. Maretti*, 321 N.W.2d 182 (Wis. 1982), a well-known case where the Wisconsin Supreme Court held that nuisance law would apply to the dispute, but remanded the matter to the trial court without deciding whether, in fact, the shadow was a nuisance.

Read the case file below to begin preparing for the negotiation. In addition to the file, your professor will give you confidential information concerning your side of the negotiation. As you work on your negotiation plan: (1) consider how the elements of a private nuisance are or are not met based on the facts provided; and (2) use this legal analysis to justify your bargaining position.

VERNA AND JAMES SINCLAIR
89 LAKESHORE WAY
DEEP SPRING, MADISON 55481

June 15, YR-00

Mr. Irwin Tarr
Quality Construction Co.
1225 Industrial Drive
Capital City, Madison 55488

Dear Mr. Tarr:

We are writing in reference to your company's plan to build a single-story home on the vacant lot located at 87 Lakeshore Way, immediately south of our home. You are probably aware that our home has a photovoltaic system which is mounted on the south-facing side of our roof. The system was installed seven years ago by Madison Solar Systems, and it currently saves us approximately $520 per month in electricity bills. We're enclosing the MSS bid for your review.

We recently learned that your proposed house will substantially block the sunshine from reaching our PV system. This is because its roof is too high and out of scale with the rest of the neighborhood. The average height for a single-story home in the Lakeshore community is 18 feet, measured at the peak of the roof line; the highest such home is only 23 feet. But the home proposed for your lot will be approximately 39 feet high at the roof line, with the chimney extending 4 feet above that point, to a total of 43 feet. There is simply no reason to build such a tall house, since there will be no inhabitable space above the ground floor—simply a very tall, empty attic.

When we asked MSS about the probable impact of this high roof on our system, we learned that the severe shadow effect would both (1) substantially reduce the efficiency of our PV system, thus increasing the cost of our electricity and (2) threaten the viability of the system itself. The letter we got from MSS about this is also enclosed.

In light of these facts, we call on you to lower the roof of your proposed home. As the MSS letter indicates, if the height of the home were reduced to a total of 28 feet (24 feet at the roof peak, plus a 4 foot chimney), it would not harm our system.

We look forward to hearing from you as soon as possible.

Sincerely,

Verna Sinclair

Jim Sinclair

MADISON SOLAR SYSTEMS, INC.

"Leading the way in energy conservation"
331 Main Street
Capital City, Madison 55490
(790) 489-2000

March 1, YR-07

Verna and Jim Sinclair
89 Lakeshore Way
Deep Spring, Madison 55481

Dear Verna and Jim:

This letter constitutes our proposal to install a solar energy system on the roof of your home at the address above. Your south-facing roof is ideal for such a system because it has approximately 350 square feet of surface area, which could accommodate a highly-efficient photovoltaic system. We propose:

Product: 24 SolarPower® solar panels

PV surface area: 337 sq. ft.

System size: 7.89 kW/month

Cost (materials and installation): $25,760 plus tax

Efficiency: will supply 94% of electricity needs

Cost savings: approximately $460 per month

Timing: installation completed by June 1, YR-07

The above cost savings analysis is based on the average monthly bill which you received from Madison Electric Enterprise during the prior year. If MEE increases its rates in future years, the annual savings would be greater. In addition, national studies consistently demonstrate that the installation of a PV system of this size will, on average, increase the fair market value of your home by approximately $19,500.

We look forward to installing your new system! This bid is valid for two weeks from the date of the letter. Please call me at your earliest convenience.

Sincerely,

Elena Cooper

Elena Cooper
Assistant Manager

MADISON SOLAR SYSTEMS, INC.

"Leading the way in energy conservation"
331 Main Street
Capital City, Madison 55490
(790) 489-2000

June 3, YR-00

Verna and Jim Sinclair
89 Lakeshore Way
Deep Spring, Madison 55481

Dear Verna and Jim:

At your request, I took a look at the plans which Quality Construction Co. filed with the city for the house it proposes to build on the south side of your lot. Based on that review, I conclude that the proposed house would have a serious negative impact on your PV system. The reason is that the proposed house will be 43 feet high (39 feet at the roof peak, plus a 4 foot chimney), which is unusually high for a single-story house.

It is difficult to quantify the precise impact of such a house on your system without an extensive analysis which takes into account the angle and elevation of the sun's rays at different times of the year. In general, however, my opinion is that the proposed house would reduce the efficiency of your system by 79%, which would on average increase your monthly electricity bill by $395 at current rates. Of course, the impact would be greater in winter and correspondingly smaller in summer, due to the position of the sun.

The other problem is that such a shadow effect might impair the integrity of the system itself. The SolarPower® panel was designed to function in environments without an extensive shadow effect, which is why it was perfect for your roof. No one could have foreseen that such a tall house would be built next door. We do not have extensive data on the viability of SolarPower® panels exposed to recurring shadows, because they were not intended for such locations. However, the partial data that does exist strongly suggests that the proposed house would reduce the useful life of your PV system by about 5 or 6 years. Right now, your system should last another 17 years, but the shadow effect would reduce it to roughly 12 to 13 years.

We would be happy to install a replacement system for you at any time! We appreciate your business. By the way, if you can convince any neighbor to install one of our systems, we will provide you with a finder's fee of $500.

Sincerely,

Elena

Elena Cooper
Manager

Ellery, Price & Wong

Attorneys at Law
30 Jefferson Square, Fifth Floor
Capital City, Madison 55492-0987
790.490.8900

July 17, YR-00

Mr. and Mrs. James Sinclair
89 Lakeshore Way
Deep Spring, Madison 55481

Dear Mr. and Mrs. Sinclair:

Our firm acts as general counsel for Quality Construction Company ("Quality") and, accordingly, your June 15 letter concerning its planned project at 87 Lakeshore Way was referred to me.

Please be advised that Quality's proposed home is fully consistent with the Deep Spring zoning ordinance and with the covenants, conditions, and restrictions ("CC&Rs") which encumber all lots in the Lakeshore community. The ordinance provides that no home in this zone may exceed 50 feet in height, while the CC&Rs merely require that any home built in the community "shall be a single-story home." The proposed home will be less than 50 feet in height and, as your letter admits, it will be a "single-story home."

You may be interested to learn that the home was designed by E.B. Zolti, the well-known Swiss architect, whose unusually tall residences have garnered architectural awards in France and Japan. The height of the home is integral to the design, and, accordingly, will allow Quality to obtain a higher purchase price for the property when it is eventually sold. As you presumably understand, Quality is building the home for sale to a buyer whose identity is not yet known.

While we naturally regret that you are unhappy with the proposed home, please understand that Quality has a right to build this home on the lot it owns in full compliance with the law. With due respect, we must point out that you could have tried to obtain a legal right to ensure the continued flow of sunshine to your roof, such as an easement or covenant, *before* you invested in your PV system. Having failed to do so, you cannot now complain when a property owner wishes to exercise its right to build.

Very truly yours,

Quinn V. Ellery

Quinn V. Ellery

110

ADAMS & BLODGETT

A Professional Corporation
102 Lakeside Court
Deep Spring, Madison 55481
(790) 392-4409

October 1, YR-00

Quinn V. Ellery, Esq.
Ellery, Price & Wong
30 Jefferson Square, Fifth Floor
Capital City, Madison 55492

Re: <u>Sinclair v. Quality Construction Co.</u>

Dear Mr. Ellery:

Verna and James Sinclair have retained our firm to represent them concerning the plan of your client Quality Construction Company to build an unusually high house on the lot immediately south of their home.

In our view, the proposed house would be an intentional private nuisance because it would cast shadow on the photovoltaic system which the Sinclairs installed on their roof some years ago. Your client has already received documentation from Madison Solar Systems, Inc. which demonstrates that the high roof on the proposed house would reduce the efficiency of the Sinclair system and shorten its useful life.

You are undoubtedly aware that the Madison Supreme Court has adopted the Restatement (Second) of Torts test for determining when such a nuisance exists. Under that standard, the proposed house constitutes a nuisance for these reasons: (a) it is intentional because your client is on notice of the harm it would cause; (b) the shadow is nontrespassory; (c) the gravity of the harm caused by the house far outweighs its utility; (d) the shadow effect would be a substantial interference with the Sinclair system; and (e) the shadow will injure the Sinclairs in their capacity as property owners.

Accordingly, the Sinclairs have authorized my firm to file suit on their behalf. As a courtesy, I am enclosing the complaint which we intend to file if this dispute cannot be resolved in a manner satisfactory to them. You will note that we intend to seek injunctive relief which will prevent your client from building the proposed house. Please contact me at your earliest convenience.

Sincerely,

Roberta C. Blodgett
Roberta C. Blodgett

DRAFT

ROBERTA C. BLODGETT
ADAMS & BLODGETT
102 Lakeside Court
Deep Spring, Madison 55481
(790) 392-4409

Attorneys for Plaintiffs

SUPERIOR COURT OF MADISON

COUNTY OF HURON

VERNA M. SINCLAIR and
JAMES P. SINCLAIR,
 	
        Plaintiffs,
 	
vs.
 	
QUALITY CONSTRUCTION
COMPANY, a Madison corporation,
and DOES 1 through 20, inclusive,
 	
        Defendants.
	No.
	
	COMPLAINT FOR INJUNCTIVE
	RELIEF AND DAMAGES

Plaintiffs allege as follows:

GENERAL ALLEGATIONS

1. Plaintiffs VERNA M. SINCLAIR and JAMES P. SINCLAIR are, and at all times mentioned herein were, the owners of fee simple absolute title in that certain real property known as 89 Lakeshore Way, Deep Spring, Huron County, Madison, consisting of a single-family residence and its accompanying lot (the "Home"). The south-facing roof of the said residence contains a photovoltaic system (the "PV System") which converts sunshine into electricity, supplying almost all of the electric power needed at the Home.

2. Plaintiffs are informed and believe, and thereon allege, that defendant QUALITY CONSTRUCTION COMPANY ("QCC") is a corporation organized and existing under the laws

of Madison, with its principal place of business in Capital City, Madison. Plaintiffs are further informed and believe, and thereon allege, that QCC is the owner of fee simple absolute title in that certain real property known as 87 Lakeshore Way, Deep Spring, Huron County, Madison (the "QCC Lot"), consisting of an unimproved lot. The QCC Lot is adjacent to, and immediately south of, the Home. Plaintiffs are further informed and believe, and thereon allege, that QCC intends to construct a house on the QCC Lot, which will be 43 feet high at its highest point, far higher than any other house in the region (the "QCC House").

3. Plaintiffs do not know the true name and capacities of the defendants sued herein as DOES 1 through 20, and will seek leave to amend this complaint to set forth the true names and capacities of these fictitiously named defendants when the same have been ascertained. Plaintiffs are informed and believe, and thereon allege, that DOES 1 through 20 were agents or employees of each of the remaining defendants, and were acting within the scope of such agency and employment in connection with the acts and omissions set forth below.

FIRST CAUSE OF ACTION
(Nuisance—Injunctive Relief)

1. Plaintiffs incorporate in full Paragraphs 1 through 3 of the General Allegations set forth above.

2. Plaintiffs are informed and believe, and thereon allege, that the QCC House will cast extensive shadow on the PV System, thereby interfering with access to the sunshine which is needed for it to function in a normal manner. This extensive shadow will greatly reduce the efficiency of the PV System and shorten its useful life.

3. The QCC House would constitute an intentional private nuisance because of the extensive shadow which it will cast on the PV System. The shadow would constitute a nontrespassory invasion of the Home, which is intentional and unreasonable, and which would substantially interfere with the normal and comfortable enjoyment of the Home.

4. On June 15, YR-00, plaintiffs gave notice in writing to QCC of the damage which the proposed QCC House would cause to the Home, but QCC has refused, and continues to refuse, to alter the design of the QCC House to avoid the harmful shadow effect.

5. QCC has threatened to and will, unless restrained by this court, proceed to construct the QCC House, in violation of the rights of the plaintiffs. Unless QCC is restrained by this court, plaintiffs will suffer irreparable injury in that the usefulness and economic value of the

Home will be substantially diminished and plaintiffs will be deprived of the comfortable enjoyment of the Home. Plaintiffs have no adequate remedy at law.

WHEREFORE, plaintiffs pray for judgment as hereinafter set forth.

SECOND CAUSE OF ACTION
(Nuisance—Damages)

1. Plaintiffs incorporate in full Paragraphs 1 through 3 of the General Allegations set forth above and Paragraphs 1 through 4 of the First Cause of Action set forth above.

2. As a proximate result of the nuisance created by QCC, the value of the Home will be substantially diminished, in an amount exceeding $50,000. Plaintiffs will seek leave to amend this complaint to set forth the exact amount of damages they have suffered when the same can be ascertained.

WHEREFORE, plaintiffs pray for judgment as follows:

1. First Cause of Action

a. For a preliminary and a permanent injunction enjoining defendants from constructing a house on the QCC Lot which causes a shadow effect that interferes with or in any way affects the normal operation of the PV System;

b. For costs of suit incurred herein;

c. For such other and further relief as the Court may deem proper.

2. Second Cause of Action

a. For compensatory damages according to proof;

b. For costs of suit incurred herein;

c. For such other and further relief as the Court may deem proper.

Dated: October ___, YR-00   ADAMS & BLODGETT

                                              By:
                                              Roberta C. Blodgett

CHAPTER 9

EASEMENTS

A. INTRODUCTION

The exercise in this chapter introduces you to the law governing easements. An *easement* is a nonpossessory right to use land owned by another. Most easements are created by an agreement between the affected parties. However, under some circumstances, an easement may be imposed as a matter of law, without the consent of the owner of the burdened land.

This is a negotiation exercise in which the owners of one parcel claim to have an easement over an adjacent parcel; the owner of the land that would be burdened denies that any easement exists. You will act as an attorney for one side in trying to negotiate a resolution of the controversy using principles of easement law.

The first section of the chapter provides an overview of relevant easement law. The next section gives you two new techniques to use in the negotiation. The final section is the case file of documents relevant to the dispute.

B. OVERVIEW OF THE LAW

The easement is a vital tool for productive use of land. Easements are often created in order to allow an owner access to her land. For example, A may need an easement to travel across B's land in order to reach A's own land. However, easements may also be necessary for cable television service, electric lines, water pipes, gas lines, sewage systems, and other purposes.

Easement law uses special terminology. All easements are either appurtenant or in gross. An *appurtenant easement* benefits the holder in her use of a specific parcel of land, called the *dominant tenement* or dominant land; the burdened land is called the *servient tenement* or servient land. The owner of the dominant tenement is called the *dominant owner*, while the owner of the servient tenement is called the *servient owner*. An *easement in gross* is not connected to the holder's use of any particular land, but rather is personal to the holder.

The most common type of easement is the *express easement*, one which is voluntarily created by the servient owner. However, depending on the circumstances, four types of easements may arise as a matter of law, without the servient owner's consent: (1) *implied easement by prior existing use*; (2) *easement by necessity*; (3) *prescriptive easement*; and (4) *easement by estoppel* (or *irrevocable license*).

In this negotiation, the parties seeking to establish an easement assert that they have either a prescriptive easement or an easement by estoppel (or irrevocable license). The requirements for these easements are discussed below.

1. *Prescriptive easement:* Although the prescriptive easement elements are similar to those required for adverse possession, the precise formula differs somewhat from state to state. One common approach requires that the claimant's use of the alleged easement be: (a) open and notorious; (b) adverse and hostile; (c) continuous; and (d) for the statutory period. You should be familiar with these elements from your study of adverse possession. In the typical case, there is little or no evidence about whether the claimant's use was adverse or permissive; the facts simply show that the owner did not object. There is a split of authority about whether the law should presume adversity or consent in this situation. Most courts presume adversity; however, some courts presume consent, especially if the land is wild and unenclosed. Madison courts have not decided this issue. However, a Madison law does provide that the statutory period to obtain a prescriptive easement is five years.

2. *Easement by estoppel* (or *irrevocable license*): The easement by estoppel arises as a matter of basic fairness when one property owner has caused another owner to change his position to his prejudice. Section 2.10(1) of the Restatement (Third) of Property: Servitudes provides that an easement or other servitude can arise by estoppel under the following circumstances:

> If injustice can be avoided only by establishment of a servitude, the owner or occupier of land is estopped to deny the existence of a servitude burdening the land when:

> (1) the owner or occupier permitted another to use that land under circumstances in which it was reasonable to foresee that the user would substantially change position believing that the permission would not be revoked, and the user did substantially change position in reasonable reliance on that belief . . . .

Some states do not recognize the easement by estoppel, but do accept the irrevocable license. There appears to be no functional difference between the two concepts. In general, an irrevocable license arises when three elements are met: (a) a landowner allows another to use his land, thus creating a license; (b) the licensee relies in good faith on the license; and (c) the licensor knows or reasonably should expect that such reliance will occur. Madison courts recognize both the easement by estoppel and the irrevocable license, using the tests set forth above.

C. NEGOTIATION TECHNIQUES

Remember the techniques you learned in earlier chapters:

1. *Develop a plan for the negotiation.*

2. *Set appropriate goals for the negotiation.*

3. *Envision the negotiation from the other side's perspective.*

4. *Develop two goals: an aspirational goal and a bottom-line goal.*

5. *Ask questions.*

6. *Revisit the plan.*

7. *Keep in mind your BATNA.*

8. *Be willing to walk away.*

9. *Negotiate from interests, not positions.*

10. *Use legitimizing sources.*

This section will introduce you to two additional techniques:

11. *Search for mutual benefit.* There is a tendency to think of a negotiation as a zero-sum game: if one side wins, the other side loses. The good negotiator searches for a creative solution that avoids the zero-sum game mindset, and thereby maximizes the outcome for her client. Focus on the interests that both sides share in the negotiation and explore ideas that serve those shared interests.

12. *Watch body language.* It is said that about 90% of human communication is nonverbal. Our bodies communicate our thoughts and feelings even when we are silent. Accordingly, a good negotiator is alert to the body language of herself and her opponent. For example, anyone who has played poker is familiar with the concept of a *tell*—an involuntary expression, gesture, movement, or body position that reflects how a player feels about the quality of his hand. The same dynamics are present in a negotiation.

D. *SANAI v. MCGUIRE*

In this exercise, Dana and Jim McGuire claim that they have an easement to cross land owned by Sabrina Sanai in order to reach Pinewood Lake. Sanai originally owned two parcels: (1) the northern parcel which adjoins the lake; and (2) the southern parcel which adjoins the highway. She sold the southern parcel to the McGuires. The McGuires now claim that they have a prescriptive easement or easement by estoppel (or irrevocable license) to cross the northern parcel. Sanai has filed a declaratory relief action, seeking a judgment that the McGuires do not have an easement.

Read the case file below as the first step in preparing for the negotiation. Your professor will provide you with confidential information for your side of the negotiation. As you work on your negotiation plan, consider how likely it is on the facts that the court will hold that the McGuires have either (1) a prescriptive easement or (2) an easement by estoppel (or irrevocable license).

SABRINA H. SANAI
350 HIGHWAY 49
PINEWOOD, MADISON

July 4

Dear Dana and Jim:

I was very sorry to shoo you and your guests off of the beach today, but after all these years it was just too much. Privacy is extremely important to me, as you well know, and those kids were making so much noise!

Maybe I haven't been careful enough about protecting my rights. I just don't know. The way I was raised, people ought to be neighborly. They should look after each other, and not raise too much of a fuss. I've tried to be a good neighbor to the two of you, surely I have, especially since you moved into your lovely new house. I know that you have been coming onto my land sometimes. But enough is enough.

So now I'm going to put this all down in writing in this letter so that there can be no misunderstanding. You cannot cross my land to get to the lake and you cannot use my beach. I suppose that I can't stop you from swimming in the lake, if you can get there somehow without crossing my land; at least, that's what my lawyer says. But you can't come onto my land any more.

I hope that this decision does not affect our friendship and that you will understand my position. My daughter tells me that I should stick up for my rights more, and I guess that I have to now.

Your neighbor,

Sabrina

128

Donald S. Middleton & Associates
57B Main Street
Pinewood, Madison 55498
(792) 890-1157

July 28, YR-00

Mrs. Sabrina H. Sanai
350 Highway 49
Pinewood, Madison 55498

Re: Easement held by Dana and James McGuire

Dear Mrs. Sanai:

Your neighbors Dana and James McGuire have asked me to represent them in connection with what appears to be a dispute about their easement to cross your land ("Parcel A") to reach Lake Pinewood. They were both shocked and embarrassed when you suddenly demanded that they and their guests leave the lake on the 4th of July. This conduct violated the easement rights held by the McGuires.

It is true that nothing was put in writing about the easement when the McGuires bought their land ("Parcel B") from you. But the law does not require that an easement be placed in written form. For eight years, the McGuires have sometimes crossed Parcel A during the summer months to reach the lake, using a path which runs through the forest on the east side of that parcel, and used the lake beach. I understand from the McGuires that you have seen them using the path on several occasions during that period, without any complaint from you. Indeed, I am told that on each occasion you waved to them politely and shouted out a friendly greeting. In addition, during the same period, the McGuires report that you saw them on the beach on at least four occasions before July 4, again without any objection from you. Because there is no public access to the lake, you clearly were aware that they had reached it via the path across Parcel A. Finally, in good faith reliance on their right to cross Parcel A and thereby enjoy the lake, the McGuires built their new house on Parcel B at a cost of $278,000. For all of these reasons and more, the McGuires hold an easement across Parcel A.

I respectfully request that you consult an attorney about this matter. Please have your attorney contact me so that we can end this dispute without the need for litigation.

Sincerely,

Donald S. Middleton
Donald S. Middleton

Bosk, Bosk & Vasquez, LLP
30 Century Plaza, Suite 2100
Capital City, Madison 55481
(792) 899-2300

August 5, YR-00

Donald S. Middleton, Esq.
57B Main Street
Pinewood, Madison 55498

Re: <u>Sabrina H. Sanai</u>

Dear Mr. Middleton:

Our client Sabrina H. Sanai has forwarded your July 28 letter to us. Please be advised that our firm regularly serves as counsel for Mrs. Sanai and her various business interests and, accordingly, we will be representing her in this matter.

At the onset, let me make it clear that my client categorically rejects the assertion that the McGuires hold an easement over her land ("Parcel A"). I am enclosing for your review the original deed by which Mrs. Sanai conveyed part of her land ("Parcel B") to the McGuires. The deed clearly shows that no easement of any kind was created by that conveyance. As your clients are well aware, Mrs. Sanai values her privacy highly; she never would have given them an easement to cross her land.

Your clients appear to be asserting that they hold an easement which is not in "written form." Yet the basis for this claim is unclear. Parcel B has access to a public road, so there can be no easement by necessity claim. Similarly, because Mrs. Sanai never used Parcel A for the benefit of Parcel B before the sale to the McGuires, there can be no implied easement by prior existing use. Next, the McGuires cannot claim a prescriptive easement, among other reasons, because their alleged use was not open and notorious, adverse and hostile, or continuous. I have personally inspected the land with two colleagues, and there is no "path" on the land, contrary to your letter; at most, there are a few places where deer or other animals have left a faint game trail. Finally, the McGuires cannot hold an easement by estoppel because Mrs. Sanai never agreed to their use and they never relied on any supposed agreement.

Very truly yours,

Ernesta A. Bosk

Ernesta A. Bosk

130

Recording requested by:
Dana X. McGuire
6231 Kronberg Park Drive
Pinewood, Madison 55498

DEED

For valuable consideration, the receipt of which is hereby acknowledged   Sabrina H. Sanai, a single woman,   **hereby grants to**

Dana X. McGuire and James B. McGuire, as joint tenants with right of survivorship,

that certain real property in the County of Evergreen,   **State of Madison described as follows:**

South half of the south half of the southeast quarter of Section 5, T3N, R5W, Madison, Fifth Principal Meridian.

Dated: January 4, YR-07   **Signed:** *Sabrina H. Sanai*

STATE OF MADISON
COUNTY OF Evergreen

On   January 4, YR-07 **before me, the undersigned,**
a notary public in and for said State, personally
appeared Sabrina H. Sanai   **personally known**
to me (or proved on the basis of satisfactory
evidence) to be the person(s) whose name(s)
is/are subscribed to the within instrument and
acknowledged to me that he/she/they executed
the same. Signed: *Harrison B. Zilner*

Bosk, Bosk & Vasquez, LLP
30 Century Plaza, Suite 2100
Capital City, Madison 55481
(792) 899-2300

October 10, YR-00

Donald S. Middleton, Esq.
57B Main Street
Pinewood, Madison 55498

Re: Sabrina H. Sanai

Dear Mr. Middleton:

This will respond to your September 15 letter.

I regret that your clients have persisted in raising baseless claims. In my August 5 letter, I explained in detail why these claims have no merit. In light of that explanation, the apparent decision of your clients to continue with their assertions seems to be slander of title, which is a tort under Madison law, as I presume you know.

You have twice threatened my client with litigation in this matter, presumably in the hope of cajoling her into giving your clients something that they are not entitled to: an easement. In order to bring an end to this harassment, my client has authorized this firm to file a declaratory relief action against your clients. I enclose a copy of the complaint, which was filed today, for your review.

Please tell me whether you are authorized to accept service of process in this matter on behalf of your clients.

Very truly yours,

Ernesta A. Bosk

Ernesta A. Bosk

ERNESTA A. BOSK
BOSK, BOSK & VASQUEZ
30 Century Plaza, Suite 2100
Capital City, Madison 55481
(792) 899-2300

Attorneys for Plaintiff
SABRINA H. SANAI

SUPERIOR COURT OF MADISON

COUNTY OF EVERGREEN

SABRINA H. SANAI,

        Plaintiff,

vs.

DANA X. McGUIRE and
JAMES B. McGUIRE,

        Defendants

No. 18-0921

COMPLAINT TO QUIET TITLE

Plaintiff SABRINA H. SANAI alleges as follows:

1. Plaintiff is, and at all times herein mentioned was, the owner in fee simple absolute of forty (40) acres of land located in Pinewood, Evergreen County, Madison ("the Property") which is legally described as follows: the north half of the south half of the southeast quarter of Section 5, T3N, R5W, Madison, Fifth Principal Meridian. The basis of plaintiff's title to the Property is a deed conveying fee simple absolute title to plaintiff dated May 1, 1990, which was recorded in the official records of Evergreen County on May 1, 1990 in Book 14, Page 602. A true and correct copy of this deed is attached hereto as Exhibit A. Plaintiff uses the Property as her personal residence.

2. Defendants Dana X. McGuire and James B. McGuire ("defendants") are, and at all times herein mentioned were, individuals residing in Pinewood, Evergreen County, Madison.

3. Plaintiff seeks to quiet title against the following claim of defendants. As set forth in the September 15, YR-00 letter from their attorney, Donald S. Middleton, to Ernesta A. Bosk, attorney for plaintiff, defendants claim an easement or irrevocable license which allegedly allows

them to travel over and across the Property. A true and correct copy of said letter is attached hereto as Exhibit B solely for the purpose of demonstrating that a dispute has arisen between plaintiff and the defendants; plaintiff does not admit that any of the allegations contained in said letter are accurate.   The precise nature and basis of the claim being made by defendants are unknown to plaintiff. It appears that defendants may be claiming a prescriptive easement, an easement by estoppel, or an irrevocable license which allegedly entitles them to travel over and across the Property.   However, defendants' claim is completely without any basis, and defendants have no right, title, estate, or interest whatsover in the Property or any part of it.

WHEREFORE, plaintiff prays for judgment as follows:

1. For a judgment quieting title to the Property in plaintiff and decreeing that defendants have no right, title, estate, or interest in the Property;

2. For costs of suit incurred herein; and

3. For such other and further relief as the Court may deem proper.

Dated: October 10, YR-00   BOSK, BOSK & VASQUEZ

Ernesta A. Bosk

Ernesta A. Bosk

Recording requested by:
Sabrina H. Sanai
350 Highway 49
Pinewood, Madison 55498

DEED

For valuable consideration, the receipt of which is hereby acknowledged, Midstate Land & Cattle Company, a Madison corporation,   hereby grants to

Sabrina H. Sanai

that certain real property in the County of   Evergreen,   State of Madison described as follows:

The south half of the southeast quarter of Section 5, T3N, R5W, Madison, Fifth Principal Meridian, comprising a parcel of eighty (80) acres

Dated: May 1, 1990   Signed: *Carl B. Knutson*
                                       President
                                       Midstate Land & Cattle Company

STATE OF MADISON
COUNTY OF   Evergreen

On   May 1, 1990   before me, the undersigned, a notary public in and for said State, personally appeared   Carl B. Knutson   personally known to me (or proved on the basis of satisfactory evidence) to be the person(s) whose name(s) is/are subscribed to the within instrument and acknowledged to me that he/she/they executed the same.

Signed: *Madeline C. Kozlow*

EXHIBIT A

Donald S. Middleton & Associates
57B Main Street
Pinewood, Madison 55498
(792) 890-1157

September 15, YR-00

Ms. Ernesta A. Bosk
Bosk, Bosk & Vasquez
30 Century Plaza, Suite 2100
Capital City, Madison 55481

Re: Easement held by Dana and James McGuire

Dear Ms. Bosk:

Thank you for your August 5 letter in this matter. I remain hopeful that we can resolve this situation without litigation. First, let me make it clear that there is indeed a path that runs from the McGuire land, across the Sanai land, and reaches Lake Pinewood, as shown on the attached map. I have personally walked on this path several times, most recently last Saturday. Your letter calls it a "faint game trail." I beg to differ. It is a clearly discernable path, which varies in width from 12 to 18 inches.

Second, the McGuires qualify for a prescriptive easement. The path itself was open and notorious, as discussed above; and your client saw them using the path on various occasions. On average, the McGuires used the path three times each month during the summer, which is a continuous use given the nature of the land. Their use was adverse and hostile based on the circumstances and because they never sought your client's permission. Finally, they used it for eight years (YR-07 to YR-00), while Madison law only requires five years.

In the alternative, the McGuires have an easement by estoppel. If no prescriptive easement is found, then your client's friendly greetings and waves can be viewed as a form of permission to use the land. The McGuires relied on this permission by building their new house on Parcel B. They would not have built on the land without having access to the lake.

I have prepared the enclosed deed of easement for your client to sign in order to resolve this situation. Because it would be expensive to draft an easement that exactly tracks the curves of the current path, I have simplified the easement route a bit. Also, note that the easement will be four feet wide, to accommodate situations where there are people going in different directions. With respect, I ask that you advise your client to execute the deed before a notary public and return it to me within two weeks.

Sincerely,

Donald S. Middleton

Donald S. Middleton

EXHIBIT B

Recording requested by:
Dana X. McGuire
332 Highway 49
Pinewood, Madison 55498

When recorded mail to:
Same

QUITCLAIM DEED

For valuable consideration,   Sabrina H. Sanai, a single woman

hereby quitclaim(s) to   Dana X. McGuire and James B. McGuire, as joint tenants with right of survivorship,

the real property located in the County of Evergreen   **State of Madison described as follows:**

an easement as described on Exhibit 1 attached hereto

Dated:_____   Signed:_____

STATE OF MADISON
COUNTY OF Evergreen

On _____, before me, the undersigned,
a notary public in and for said State, personally
appeared Sabrina H. Sanai   **personally known**
to me (or proved on the basis of satisfactory
evidence) to be the person(s) whose name(s)
is/are subscribed to the within instrument and
acknowledged to me that he/she/they executed
the same.

Signed: _____

EXHIBIT 1

An easement for ingress and egress over and across a strip of land four (4) feet in width on the north half of the south half of the southeast quarter of Section 5, T3N, R5W, Madison, Fifth Principal Meridian, which strip of land is located immediately west of the following described line: starting at the red iron pole located on the north boundary line of the south half of the south half of the southeast quarter of Section 5, T3N, R5W, Madison, Fifth Principal Meridian, thence 15 degrees east of north for 290 feet, thence 30 degrees west of north for 352 feet, thence 50 degrees east of north for 307 feet, thence 4 degrees east of north for approximately 300 feet until the said line intersects the mean high water mark of Lake Pinewood.

Said easement is appurtenant to and for the benefit of the south half of the south half of the southeast quarter of Section 5, T3N, R5W, Madison, Fifth Principal Meridian.

An approximate map of the location of said easement is attached. In the event of any inconsistency between the said map and the legal description above, the said description shall control.

Map of Easement Location
Note: Not to scale. For illustration only.

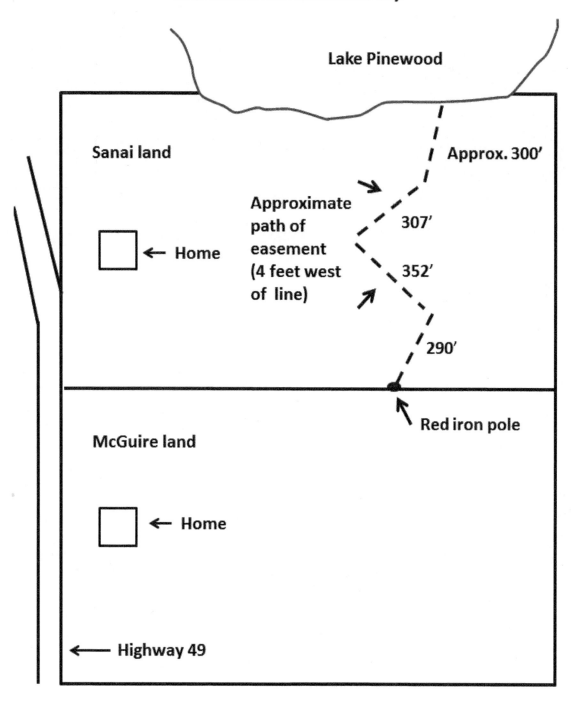

Lake Pinewood

Sanai land

Approx. 300'

Approximate path of easement (4 feet west of line)

307'

352'

← Home

290'

Red iron pole

McGuire land

← Home

← Highway 49

CHAPTER 10

COVENANTS, CONDITIONS, AND RESTRICTIONS

A. INTRODUCTION

The exercise in this chapter involves private land use restrictions. It is increasingly common for new housing developments to be subject to such restrictions because of the benefits they provide. For example, a requirement that all the lots in a subdivision be used for residential purposes gives buyers the assurance that no one can build a noisy factory next door.

This is an advocacy exercise about the enforceability of a private land use restriction in a residential subdivision. You will act as an attorney making a closing argument to the judge in a court trial after the testimony has been completed, representing either the homeowner or the association charged with enforcing the restriction.

The first section of this chapter examines the law governing the enforceability of these restrictions. The next section is the case file for the exercise. You may want to review Chapter 2, Section C, which discusses the procedural aspects of a closing argument after a court trial.

B. OVERVIEW OF THE LAW

Traditionally, it was difficult to create a private land use restriction that would bind and benefit future owners. Somewhat grudgingly, the English law courts eventually recognized the *real covenant*, which allowed the benefits and burdens of a restriction to "run with the land" to successive owners. But they imposed a complex set of requirements that curtailed its use. A similar device—the *equitable servitude*—evolved in the English equity courts, with less stringent requirements.

Modern law favors the creation of private land use restrictions. Over 60 million Americans live in privately-planned communities such as housing tracts, townhouse developments, condominium projects, and entire private towns. These communities are regulated by land use restrictions known as *covenants, conditions, and restrictions (CC&Rs)*. CC&Rs are enforced using the traditional tools of real covenants and equitable servitudes. Today, disputes rarely arise about whether particular CC&Rs were validly created. The law has evolved to the point where it is fairly simple for a developer to create binding CC&Rs. The more difficult question is whether a unit owner has a defense to enforcement.

While most CC&Rs are mundane, some are controversial because they are seen as unduly interfering with the freedom of individual owners. Critics argue that because the typical buyer does not read the CC&Rs before he purchases his unit, he should not be bound by them; they also express concern that intrusive CC&Rs are inconsistent with our tradition of respecting personal liberty inside the home. Supporters of CC&Rs, in contrast, stress that (1) each unit owner voluntarily accepts the restrictions by the act of purchasing his unit and (2) enforcement is necessary to protect the legitimate interests of other unit owners. As a Florida court summarized in *Hidden Harbour Estates, Inc. v. Norman*, 309 So. 2d 180, 181-82 (Fla. Dist. Ct. App. 1975), "inherent in the condominium concept is the principle that to promote the health, happiness, and peace of mind of the majority of the unit owners since they are living in such close proximity and using facilities in common, each unit owner must give up a certain degree of freedom of choice . . . ."

American courts are gradually developing an approach to the enforceability of CC&Rs that strikes a compromise between these views. One of the leading decisions in the area is *Nahrstedt v. Lakeside Village Condominium Association, Inc.*, 878 P.2d 1275 (Cal. 1994), which examined the validity of a restriction banning cats, dogs, and other pets. After the homeowners' association assessed fines against her for having three cats in her condominium unit, Nahrstedt filed an action seeking a declaration that the restriction was "unreasonable" and hence unenforceable. She relied on a state statute which provided that CC&Rs were enforceable unless they were "unreasonable." Nahrstedt asserted that because her three cats were always kept inside her unit and did not bother neighbors, it was unreasonable to ban them. She lost in the trial court on demurrer, won in the court of appeal, but finally lost in the California Supreme Court.

The *Nahrstedt* court emphasized the importance of enforcing CC&Rs in order to protect buyers who relied on them in deciding to purchase their units. Accordingly, it interpreted the statutory standard narrowly, holding that a restriction was unenforceable only if it:

(a) was arbitrary;

(b) imposed burdens on the use of land that substantially outweighed the restriction's benefits; or

(c) violated a fundamental public policy.

The court explained that an "arbitrary" restriction was one which had no "rational relationship to the protection, preservation, operation or purpose of the affected land." 878 P.2d at 1286. The court also observed that the reasonableness of a particular restriction should be assessed by reference to the development as a whole, not the particular facts relating to the complaining owner. Thus, the specific facts about Nahrstedt's three cats were irrelevant. Applying its new standard, the court held that the pet ban was valid.

C. *BURNS v. RIVERBEND VILLAGE ASSOCIATION*

The dispute in the exercise below is about the enforceability of a restriction that prohibits watching television and other electronic devices. Section 6.21 of the CC&Rs which regulate the Riverbend Village subdivision effectively bans the use of televisions and other devices. The broad language in that section also prohibits the use of computers, tablets, wireless phones, and similar devices, even though the drafters presumably did not have them in mind when the CC&Rs were adopted in 1988.

Lia Burns, one of the homeowners, has filed a suit seeking a declaratory judgment that Section 6.21 is unenforceable. The defendant in the action is the Riverbend Village Association, the entity charged with enforcing the CC&Rs. Madison courts have adopted the *Nahrstedt* standard discussed above for evaluating the enforceability of CC&Rs.

The trial testimony has concluded, and the closing arguments will begin soon. Depending on what your professor decides, you may be an attorney for Burns, an attorney for the Association, or a judge. As an attorney, your job is to explain why your client should prevail in the case, considering both the law and the facts.

The complete case file is below. It includes the complaint, the answer, and a partial transcript of the trial testimony. Both sides have access to the same facts in this exercise.

RIVERBEND VILLAGE ASSOCIATION
702 RIVER ROAD
FAIRFIELD, MADISON 55409
(790) 553-0926

January 12, YR-01

Ms. Lia Burns
23 Monet Way
Fairfield, Madison 55409

Dear Lia:

As you are well aware, Section 6.21 of the Riverbend Village CC&Rs provides that no one may watch television in the Village.

Unfortunately, last evening around 10:12 p.m. one of our security guards noticed a blue glow emanating from the windows of your home and, upon closer investigation, determined that there was reason to believe that you might be watching television—again. When he knocked on the door to inquire, you admitted that you were indeed watching a television show.

The Board has asked me to give you yet another polite warning that such conduct will not be tolerated in our community. If this conduct is repeated, the Board will need to consider whether some sort of formal sanction is required.

As the CC&Rs provide, the Village is dedicated to enriching the human spirit through traditional, family-friendly activities which characterized life in small towns before television arrived on the scene. Obviously, some people would prefer not to live in a community with this goal. But you voluntarily made the choice to do so. For the good of our community, I urge you to comply with the CC&Rs that you have pledged to obey.

With best wishes,

Bob

Bob Nielson
Board President

RIVERBEND VILLAGE ASSOCIATION

202 RIVER ROAD
FAIRFIELD, MADISON 55409
(790) 553-0926

March 31, YR-01

Ms. Lia Burns
23 Monet Way
Fairfield, Madison 55409

Dear Lia:

I'm sure you know what this letter is about.

The guard caught you watching television again two nights ago. After he saw the glow, he knocked on your door and asked if you were watching, and you conceded you were.

The Board met last night to consider your situation. We cannot uphold the integrity of the CC&Rs, and the concept of a community based on life in the pre-television era, if some feel free to ignore the restrictions. Accordingly, the Board has decided to fine you the sum of $1,000 for violating Section 6.21 of the CC&Rs. Please deliver your check, made payable to the Association, to me within 10 days from the date of this letter.

The Board also asked me to inform you that if you violate Section 6.21 in the future, progressively larger fines will be imposed on you until these violations finally stop.

With best wishes,

Bob

Bob Nielson
Board President

LINDSEY S. YOUNG
CENTER FOR HOMEOWNERS' RIGHTS
2045 Central Avenue, Suite 3K
Capital City, Madison 55465
792.445.0988

Attorneys for Plaintiff LIA V. BURNS

SUPERIOR COURT OF MADISON

COUNTY OF FREMONT

LIA V. BURNS,

          Plaintiff,   No. 15-089

vs.

RIVERBEND VILLAGE ASSOCIATION,   COMPLAINT

          Defendant.

      Plaintiff alleges as follows:

      1. Plaintiff LIA V. BURNS is an individual residing in Fremont County, Madison. Plaintiff owns a fee simple absolute title in a single-family residence located at 23 Monet Way, Fairfield, Fremont County, Madison ("Home") which is her principal place of residence. Plaintiff purchased the Home in 2005. The Home is located within a subdivision known as "Riverbend Village" ("Subdivision").

      2. Defendant RIVERBEND VILLAGE ASSOCIATION ("ASSOCIATION") is a nonprofit corporation, organized under the laws of Madison. The Board of Directors of the ASSOCIATION ("Board") is charged with certain duties and obligations concerning the Subdivision, including enforcement of legal and valid covenants, conditions, and restrictions which affect that Subdivision.

      3. On September 14, 1988, Riverbend Village Properties, Inc., which held title to the Subdivision, caused to be recorded in the chain of title to the Subdivision, including the Home, a document entitled "Declaration of Covenants, Conditions, and Restrictions" ("CC&Rs"). Excerpts from the CC&Rs are attached hereto as Exhibit A. Section 6.21 of the CC&Rs purports to prohibit anyone from watching television within the Subdivision.

4. On or about March 29, YR-01, an employee of the ASSOCIATION approached plaintiff's Home at approximately 10:35 p.m. and accused her of watching television in violation of Section 6.21. Subsequently, on March 30, YR-01, the Board imposed a fine of $1,000 on plaintiff for allegedly watching television.

5. An actual controversy has now arisen and now exists between plaintiff and the ASSOCIATION, in that:

> A. Plaintiff contends that Section 6.21 is unenforceable under Madison law because it is arbitrary, imposes burdens on the use of the lands it affects which substantially outweigh any benefits to affected Subdivision residents, and violates fundamental public policies; whereas

> B. Plaintiff is informed and believes, and thereon alleges, that the ASSOCIATION contends that Section 6.21 is enforceable.

WHEREFORE, plaintiff prays for judgment as follows:

1. For a judgment of this Court that Section 6.21 is unenforceable;

2. For costs of suit incurred herein;

3. For such other and further relief as the Court may deem proper.

Dated: June 15, YR-01   CENTER FOR HOMEOWNERS' RIGHTS

                                                       By: *Lindsey S. Young*
                                                       Lindsey S. Young

Excerpts from

DECLARATION OF COVENANTS, CONDITIONS, AND RESTRICTIONS

RIVERBEND VILLAGE

RECITALS

A. Declarant Riverbend Village Properties, Inc. ("RVP") is the owner in fee simple absolute of that certain real property located in Fairfield, Fremont County, Madison described as Parcels 1 through 101 as shown on that certain Parcel Map of "Riverbend Village" recorded on August 1, 1988, in Book 41 of Parcel Maps at Page 108, in the Office of the County Recorder of Fremont County ("Subdivision").

B. RVP intends to offer Parcels 1 through 100 in the Subdivision for sale to the general public, while Parcel 101 ("Common Area") consists of common area which shall be dedicated for use by all future owners. The purpose of this Declaration of Covenants, Conditions, and Restrictions ("Declaration") is to ensure that the owners who purchase properties in the Subdivision in the future will enjoy the unique benefits of a true community—a place dedicated to enriching the human spirit through facilitating the traditional, family-friendly activities which characterized life in small towns in the United States before the advent of television, such as community dinners, live concerts and other cultural events, outdoor games, and similar activities. It must be assumed that all persons who become owners of property subject to these CC&Rs are motivated by this goal, and accordingly accept the principle that the future development and use of the Subdivision must be consistent with it.

C. RVP hereby declares that the Subdivision, and every part thereof, shall be held, sold and conveyed subject to the following covenants, conditions, and restrictions, which are expressly intended to benefit and burden the Subdivision and which shall run with the Subdivision as among the owners thereof. These covenants, conditions, and restrictions shall be binding on all parties having any right, title, or interest in the Subdivision, or any part thereof, their heirs, successors, and assigns, and shall inure to the benefit of all such parties. Any owner of any portion of the Subdivision may enforce these covenants, conditions, and restrictions as real covenants, equitable servitudes, or otherwise.

ARTICLE 1: RIVERBEND VILLAGE ASSOCIATION

1.01   Organization: The Riverbend Village Association ("Association"), a non-profit corporation organized under the laws of Madison, is charged with the duties and empowered with the rights set forth in the provisions below. Each record owner of a fee simple estate in any parcel within the Subdivision ("Owner") shall be a member of the Association and shall have one vote on all matters submitted for a vote to the membership of the Association. The Owners shall annually elect a Board of Directors ("Board") which shall carry out the duties listed below.

1.02   Duties of the Board: The Board shall have the following duties:

EXHIBIT A

a. The Board shall maintain the Common Area, including all recreational facilities, paths, and other improvements thereon, for the benefit of all Owners and their families;

b. The Board shall take any action as may be reasonably necessary to enforce the covenants, conditions, restrictions, and other provisions of this Declaration, including, but not limited to, levying fines against any Owner who violates this Declaration or any portion thereof, and bringing suit as may be necessary against any such Owner;

c. The Board will sponsor an extensive series of community events each year within the Subdivision as it deems appropriate, in its sole discretion, to implement the purposes of this Declaration, including, but not limited to: community dinners, dances, discussions, lectures, and sing-a-longs; concerts, art exhibits, plays, poetry readings, and book clubs; and community games, fairs, markets, service projects, and similar activities.

*   *   *   *   *

ARTICLE 6: USE RESTRICTIONS

6.01   Residential Use: Each parcel in the Subdivision shall be used exclusively for single-family residential purposes, except that any Owner or a family member thereof may conduct a private business within his/her home for the limited purpose of giving lessons on cultural topics, such as art, dance, or music lessons, to individuals on a one-on-one basis so long as said business does not adversely affect the Owners of nearby parcels or their families with respect to traffic, noise, or similar issues.

6.02   Community Activities: To ensure that all Owners and their families are ready, willing, and able to participate in community activities within the Subdivision, in order to fulfill the purpose of this Declaration, restrictions are imposed below on the ability of Owners and their families to engage in certain activities which are inconsistent with this goal. It is agreed and understood that the failure or refusal of any Owner to actively participate in community activities harms all other Owners.

*   *   *   *   *

6.21   Television: No one may watch, look at, see, or otherwise utilize television in the Subdivision. As used herein, "television" means any electronic images of any kind or nature whatsoever, including but not limited to, any electronic images received or transmitted in any manner, whether viewed on a television screen or any other device, however denominated, which is capable of displaying electronic images, whether it now exists or is invented in the future. However, nothing contained herein shall be deemed to prevent anyone from listening to an electronically-created audio signal from a radio or similar device.

EXHIBIT A

CASEY D. ZATKIN
ZATKIN & MAY
552 Main Street
Fairfield, Madison 55410
(790) 778-0983

Attorneys for Defendant
RIVERBEND VILLAGE ASSOCIATION

SUPERIOR COURT OF MADISON

COUNTY OF FREMONT

LIA V. BURNS,

          Plaintiff,   No. 15-089

vs.

RIVERBEND VILLAGE ASSOCIATION,   ANSWER

          Defendant.

Defendant RIVERBEND VILLAGE ASSOCIATION answers the Complaint herein as follows:

1. Defendant admits the allegations set forth in Paragraphs 1, 2, 3, and 4.

2. Answering the allegations set forth in Paragraph 5, defendant admits that a controversy has arisen between it and plaintiff concerning the enforceability of Section 6.21, and affirmatively alleges that said section is fully valid and enforceable. Except as expressly admitted above, defendant denies each and every remaining allegation set forth in said paragraph.

WHEREFORE, defendant prays for judgment as follows:

1. For a judgment of this Court that Section 6.21 is enforceable;

2. For costs of suit incurred herein;

3. For such other and further relief as the Court may deem proper.

Dated: July 8, YR-01   ZATKIN & MAY

                                    By: *Casey D. Zatkin*
                                    Casey D. Zatkin

SUPERIOR COURT OF MADISON

2   COUNTY OF FREMONT

3

4   LIA V. BURNS,

5   Plaintiff,

6   vs.   No. 15-089

7   RIVERBEND VILLAGE ASSOCIATION,

8   Defendant.

9

10   EXCERPTS FROM TRIAL TRANSCRIPT

11   NOVEMBER 8, YR-00

12   BEFORE THE HON. LYDIA F. HOLLISTER

13   For the plaintiff: LINDSEY S. YOUNG, CENTER FOR HOMEOWNERS' RIGHTS

14   For the defendant: CASEY D. ZATKIN, ZATKIN & MAY

15   *   *   *   *   *

16   THE COURT: I understand that both sides have stipulated to the admission of Exhibit A

17   to the Complaint in this action, the excerpts from the CC&Rs. Ms. Young, you may call your

18   first witness.

19   YOUNG: Your honor, we call Lia Burns.

20   LIA V. BURNS

21   called as a witness by the plaintiff, being first duly sworn, was examined and testified as follows:

22   DIRECT EXAMINATION

23   YOUNG: Lia, please state your full name for the record.

24   A. It's Lia Victoria Burns. B-U-R-N-S.

25   Q. Let's return to January 11 of last year. Did anything unusual happen on that day?

26   A. Yes. I was sitting in my house watching television, when one of the guards...we have

27   security guards in the subdivision...he knocked on my front door and complained that I was

28   watching TV.

29   Q. Why would he do that?

30   A. Well, my house is in the Riverbend Village subdivision, and we have CC&Rs. One

31   says that no one can even watch TV. So that's why the guard came by, because he said I was

1 violating that CC&R by watching TV. And this wasn't the first time something like this

2 happened.

3   Q. Let's focus on January 11. Did you ever hear anything more about this incident?

4   A. Yes. First I got a letter from Bob Nielson, the president of the association board. I

5 suppose you would call it a warning letter. It basically told me not to watch TV any more. And

6 then I got another letter fining me $1,000 for watching TV another time.

7   Q. Lia, I now show you a document that has been admitted into evidence as Exhibit A.

8 Do you recognize it?

9   A. Yes. These are excerpts from the CC&Rs. Section 6.21, down there at the bottom of

10 the second page, that's the one I was talking about, the one that says no one can watch TV.

11   Q. Is there any connection, any relationship between section 6.21 and the protection,

12 preservation, operation or purpose of the subdivision?

13   ZATKIN: Objection, your honor. That question calls for a legal conclusion.

14   YOUNG: Your honor, Ms. Burns owns a home in the subdivision. She is entitled to

15 testify from her personal knowledge about whether there is such a relationship.

16   THE COURT: I'll allow the question.

17   A. No, there's no connection, none. The subdivision is a place for people to live, and

18 people like to watch TV in their homes. Having a TV ban, that makes no sense.

19   Q. Does the TV ban impose any burden on you and other owners in the subdivision?

20   A. It sure does. Look, watching TV is entertainment. It lets me unwind after a long, hard

21 day at work. Sometimes, I really need that for my mental health. I think all the owners do. TV

22 is also educational. I watch the news all the time on the local PBS station, so I'm always up to

23 date on politics and so forth. Sure, the CC&Rs say you can listen to radio, but the pictures you

24 can see on the TV news really tell the story. You can't get that from radio. There are lots of kids

25 in the subdivision who can't watch educational TV programming because of the ban. You can't

26 even use a computer, a tablet, or a modern phone, because those supposedly count as TV also,

27 because they have a screen. No one can use the internet. Electronic books...you can't read those

28 either.

29   Q. Does the TV ban have any benefits for you and the other owners?

1   A. No, I don't see any. They claim that if you're not watching TV, then you would be

2 out participating in dinners, concerts, games and so forth. But that's not true. Not many people

3 actually do that. Most people just read a book—an old-fashioned paper book.

4   Q. Would you say that the burden of the ban outweighs its benefits?

5   ZATKIN: Objection, your honor. Calls for a legal conclusion.

6   THE COURT: Sustained. Move on, counsel.

7   YOUNG: Does the ban affect your ability to exercise your right to free speech?

8   ZATKIN: Your honor, again, this calls for a legal conclusion.

9   THE COURT: Overruled. I'll allow it.

10   A. It limits me quite a bit. I'm deprived of most of the sources from which people get

11 information today, such as television and the internet. So I feel I'm not as informed as other

12 people are for things like making good decisions on candidates and issues. Also the internet is

13 where a lot of political discussions and debate takes place. It's kind of like a town meeting. And

14 I can't participate in that at all.

15   Q. Does the ban affect your right to privacy?

16   A. I feel that a person should be free to do anything she wants in the privacy of her own

17 home, as long as this doesn't hurt anyone else. If I want to eat oatmeal or wear odd clothes or

18 watch TV or anything else, I should be allowed to do that. I think that's part of our American

19 tradition, to be free inside the home without the government telling you what you can and can't

20 do. And the board is kind of like a government. It shouldn't be able to dictate what I do.

21   Q. Did you know that the CC&Rs banned television before you bought your house?

22   A. No, I didn't. I may have seen the CC&Rs before I bought it. I don't remember

23 exactly. But when I moved in, I brought my TV with me, so I must have thought I could use it.

24 I sure don't remember knowing at the time that there was a ban on television.

25   YOUNG: Your honor, I have no further questions.

26   THE COURT: Any cross-examination?

27   CROSS-EXAMINATION

28   ZATKIN: Yes, your honor. Ms. Burns, before you bought your house, you knew that

29 there were CC&Rs which applied to the subdivision, right?

30   A. Yes, I guess so.

31   Q. But you never even read them?

1   A. As I said, I might have read them...or looked them over. But I don't remember

2   knowing that you couldn't watch television.

3   Q. Now the CC&Rs provide that they can be amended by a majority vote of the

4   homeowners, don't they?

5   A. Yes, they do.

6   Q. But you never tried to convince anyone to get the CC&Rs amended to eliminate

7   section 6.21, did you?

8   A. No. They probably wouldn't agree.

9   Q. What do you mean by that?

10   A. Most of them, the other owners, are OK with having no television. I don't think they

11   would vote to change it.

12   Q. Ms. Burns, do you own a computer of any kind?

13   A. Yes, I have a laptop.

14   Q. And isn't it true that you can use that laptop whenever you are outside of the

15   subdivision?

16   A. Yes.

17   Q. And do you ever use it outside of the subdivision?

18   A. Sure. There's a Starbucks a few blocks away where I go regularly. I can get on the

19   internet there. A lot of other owners go there to do the same thing.

20   Q. And when you use your computer outside of the subdivision, you can get access to TV

21   programs, right?

22   A. Yes.

23   Q. And anything else on the internet, right?

24   A. Yes.

25   Q. So the television ban inside the subdivision really doesn't have much impact on you,

26   does it?

27   YOUNG: Objection, your honor. The witness already testified about the impact.

28   THE COURT: Counsel, this is cross-examination. I'll allow the question.

29   A. No, it does have a big impact on me, just like I said before.

30   Q. You could avoid the television ban by selling your house and moving somewhere else,

31   right?

154

1   A. Yes, I could. But I like the house I have now.

2   ZATKIN: Your honor, I have nothing further at this time.

3   *   *   *   *   *

4   THE COURT: Now that the plaintiff has rested, we'll hear from the defendant. Mr.

5   Zatkin, you may call your first witness.

6   ZATKIN: Your honor, I call Robert Nielson.

7   ROBERT B. NIELSON

8   called as a witness by the defendant, being duly sworn, was examined and testified as follows:

9   ZATKIN: Mr. Nielson, please state your full name for the record.

10   A. It's Bob...Robert...Nielson. That's N-i-e-l-s-o-n.

11   Q. What is your occupation?

12   A. Well, I was a high school teacher. I taught literature at Fairfield High School. But

13   I'm retired. Today I spend most of my time working for free as the president of the board of

14   directors of the association. That's the Riverbend Village Association.

15   Q. Do you know Lia Burns?

16   A. Yes, of course. She lives at 23 Monet Way, just three houses down from me. I'm at

17   17 Monet. I've known her for years.

18   Q. Now I show you a document which has been admitted into evidence as Exhibit A in

19   this case, the Declaration of Covenants, Conditions, and Restrictions for Riverbend Village. Do

20   you recognize that document?

21   A. Yes. These are the CC&Rs for our subdivision.

22   Q. And are you familiar with section 6.21 of Exhibit A?

23   A. Yes, I suppose. That's the section that prohibits television and so forth.

24   Q. Is there any relationship between section 6.21 and the protection, preservation,

25   operation or purpose of the subdivision?

26   YOUNG: Objection, your honor. That calls for a legal conclusion.

27   ZATKIN: Your honor, Ms. Young asked almost an identical question of her own

28   witness, which you allowed. I should be able to do the same thing.

29   THE COURT: Ms. Young, you opened this door. Both sides can ask the question.

30   Overruled.

1   A. Yes, there sure is. We know that our subdivision is not for everyone. As the CC&Rs

2   say, it's intended for people who want to experience life as it was before television existed,

3   where residents had the time and inclination to participate actively in community events, events

4   like dances, group discussions, plays, dinners, and others mentioned in the CC&Rs. These are

5   the kind of events where people get to talk with each other, interact with each other, as

6   persons—not where someone just sits staring at an electronic screen. If people were allowed to

7   just sit and watch a screen, they would be much less likely to participate in these community

8   events, and the rest of us would suffer from their absence.

9   Q. Does section 6.21 provide any benefits to owners in the subdivision?

10   A. Yes, like I just said. Everyone benefits from being able to participate in these

11   community events, to interact with actual people, to have real live friends. By participating in

12   live events, people learn more and just enjoy life more. Life is more real, more vibrant, more

13   fun. A machine can never substitute for a person.

14   Q. Does that section impose any burdens on owners in the subdivision?

15   A. Sure, I guess there's some restriction. If owners want to access the internet or watch

16   TV or so forth, they have to go outside the subdivision. Some of them go to Starbucks or a

17   similar place. Or they see a movie at a theater. Or they use the internet at work. But I don't see

18   that as much of a burden.

19   Q. Does section 6.21 interfere with anyone's right to free speech?

20   YOUNG: Your honor, I do have to object. This clearly asks for a legal conclusion.

21   THE COURT: Ms. Young, again, you asked a similar question so I'll allow it.

22   A. All of us in the subdivision can keep up pretty well on the news by reading the paper

23   and listening to the radio. You don't need TV or the internet for that. And, frankly, the quality

24   of news you get on TV or the internet isn't very good. Now if someone wants to send messages

25   on the internet, or use a wireless phone, they can do that just by leaving the subdivision.

26   Q. Does section 6.21 interfere with anyone's right to privacy?

27   A. No. I know that Lia says she should be able to do whatever she wants in her own

28   house. But the CC&Rs limit what she can do. She should have read them before she bought the

29   house. And if she didn't read them, that's her problem. To me, the television ban really doesn't

30   relate to privacy at all. It's just one of the many things that you can't do inside a house.

31   ZATKIN: Your honor, I have no more questions.

156

1   THE COURT: Cross-examination?

2   CROSS-EXAMINATION

3   YOUNG: Yes, your honor. The CC&Rs allow residents to watch television, use

4 computers, and so forth, as long as they leave the subdivision to do so, right?

5   A. Yes. Nothing in the CC&Rs says that they can't.

6   Q. And when residents are outside of the subdivision, then they're not available to

7 participate in community events, right?

8   A. Yes.

9   Q. Then doesn't the television ban have the effect of making people unavailable for

10 community events because it makes them leave the subdivision?

11   A. I'm not sure how to answer that. I don't think so. Right now, residents don't spend

12 too much time outside of the subdivision doing those things. But without the ban, they would

13 spend a lot more time inside their houses and be more unavailable for events.

14   Q. Sir, you own a car, don't you?

15   A. Yes, I have a Ford I bought last year.

16   Q. And it has an electronic dashboard display, doesn't it?

17   A. Yes, it does.

18   Q. And you drive your car within the subdivision, don't you?

19   A. Yes.

20   Q. You're watching the dashboard display while driving, right?

21   A. Yes, in a way. I mainly keep my eyes on the road.

22   Q. Then aren't you violating section 6.21 by watching electronic images on a device?

23   A. What do you mean?

24   Q. Isn't the electronic dashboard display covered by section 6.21?

25   A. I don't know. No one ever suggested that.

26   Q. Wouldn't it be ridiculous for CC&Rs to ban someone from driving a car?

27   ZATKIN: Objection, your honor. Calls for speculation.

28   YOUNG: I'll withdraw the question. I have no more questions at this time.

29   *   *   *   *   *

30   THE COURT: Let the record reflect that both sides have rested. We'll adjourn now and

31 reconvene in 15 minutes for closing statements.

CHAPTER 11

EMINENT DOMAIN

A. INTRODUCTION

The Takings Clause of the Fifth Amendment provides: "[N]or shall private property be taken for public use, without just compensation." It is generally accepted that the Founders viewed the power of government to take property as an inherent attribute of sovereignty. The Takings Clause imposes two restrictions on this power: (1) government may take property only for "public use"; and (2) it must pay "just compensation" to the owner.

The exercise in this chapter is a closing argument to the judge after an eminent domain trial. The city brought an action to condemn land owned by a farmer, who asserts that the proposed condemnation is not a taking for public use.

The first section of the chapter provides an overview of the public use requirement. The next section is the case file for the exercise. You may want to review Chapter 2, Section C, which discusses the procedural aspects of a closing argument in a court trial.

B. OVERVIEW OF THE LAW

Governments often need to acquire property from private owners who are unwilling to sell voluntarily for uses such as parks, highways, and schools. If government did not have the power to take property by eminent domain, an owner could flatly refuse to sell the land needed for a vital project or demand an exorbitant purchase price.

The meaning of "public use" in the Takings Clause has evolved over time. For much of our nation's history, courts interpreted the standard as requiring that the property be taken for physical use by government (e.g., a military base) or by the public (e.g., a park). However, in *Berman v. Parker*, 348 U.S. 26 (1954), the Supreme Court held that the condemnation of privately-owned land in order to redevelop slum areas was a taking for public use, even if the land would later be sold or leased to private parties. Writing for the Court, Justice Douglas focused on the *purpose* for the taking: "Once the object is within the authority of Congress, the right to realize it through the exercise of eminent domain is merely the means to the end." *Id.* at 33.

Thirty years later, the Court solidified the *Berman* approach in *Hawaii Housing Authority v. Midkiff*, 467 U.S. 229 (1984). The case arose because most fee simple land in Hawaii was held by a handful of owners, who were only willing to lease it. The legislature adopted a statute to remedy this problem; it allowed tenants living in single-family homes on such lands to petition a state agency to have these properties condemned and then resold to the tenants. In response to a lawsuit attacking the legality of the statute, the Supreme Court held that the law authorized a taking of property for public use because it would serve a public purpose: regulating the "social and economic evils of a land oligopoly." *Id.* at 241–42. The Court stressed that a taking for a public *purpose* satisfied the public use requirement: "[W]here the exercise of the eminent domain power is rationally related to a conceivable public purpose, the Court has never held a compensated taking to be proscribed by the Public Use Clause." *Id.* at 241. Finally, the Court emphasized that whether a particular taking would in fact achieve the intended goal was irrelevant. Rather, the appropriate standard was whether "the...[state] Legislature *rationally could have believed* that the [Act] would promote its objective." *Id.* at 242.

The most recent case on the question is *Kelo v. City of New London*, 545 U.S. 469 (2005), where the Supreme Court held that the city's condemnation of owner-occupied homes and other properties for the purpose of economic redevelopment was a public use, even though the city planned to convey the properties to private developers. Five members of the Court joined the majority opinion, including Justice Kennedy, who wrote a separate concurring opinion.

For four members of the majority, *Kelo* was a relatively easy case that was controlled by *Berman* and *Midkiff*. Through its redevelopment entity, the city planned to acquire title to a large region which included 115 privately-owned properties, and then transfer the land to private entities that would build facilities including a hotel, restaurants, shops, marinas, homes, offices, parking, and related uses. The city had conducted a comprehensive study which showed that the project would create more than 1,000 jobs, increase tax revenues, and revitalize the local economy. In his majority opinion, Justice Stevens observed that the city's redevelopment plan "unquestionably serves a public purpose." *Id.* at 484. Stevens rejected the landowners' suggestion that the Court should adopt "a new bright-line rule that economic development does not qualify as a public use." *Id.* He explained that promoting economic development was a "traditional and long-accepted function of government." *Id.*

Justice Kennedy's concurring opinion noted that "transfers intended to confer benefits on particular, favored private entities, and with only incidental or pretextual public benefits, are forbidden by the Public Use Clause." *Id.* at 490. However, he reasoned that this situation was not present on the *Kelo* facts:

> This is not the occasion for conjecture as to what sort of cases might justify a more demanding standard, but it is appropriate to underscore aspects of the instant case that convince me no departure from *Berman* and *Midkiff* is appropriate here. This taking occurred in the context of a comprehensive development plan meant to address a serious city wide depression, and the

projected economic benefits of the project cannot be characterized as *de minimis*. The identities of most of the private beneficiaries were unknown at the time the city formulated its plans. The city complied with elaborate procedural requirements that facilitate review of the record and inquiry into the city's purposes. In sum, while there may be categories of cases in which the transfers are so suspicious, or the procedures employed so prone to abuse, or the purported benefits are so trivial or implausible, that courts should presume an impermissible private purpose, no such circumstances are present in this case . . . .

Id. at 493.

The four *Kelo* dissenters argued that the majority had misunderstood the holdings in *Berman* and *Midkiff*, because in both cases the precondemnation use of the properties at issue had "inflicted affirmative harm on society." *Id.* at 500. Because the *Kelo* properties did not cause any such harm, they argued, the public use requirement was not met. The dissenters warned that the majority decision would have serious consequences:

[A]ll private property is now vulnerable to being taken and transferred to another private owner, so long as it might be upgraded—*i.e.*, given to an owner who will use it in a way that the legislature deems more beneficial to the public—in the process
. . . .

The specter of condemnation hangs over all property. Nothing is to prevent the State from replacing any Motel 6 with a Ritz-Carlton, any home with a shopping mall, or any farm with a factory . . . .

Id. at 494, 503.

C. *CITY OF TUSCULUM v. SMALL*

The dispute in the exercise below is whether the public use requirement is satisfied on the facts of the case. The City of Tusculum has filed an eminent domain action to condemn farm land owned by Edward Small, so that it can convey the land to the Tusculum Towers Casino Corporation. The Corporation will use the land as parking for new facilities that will be built in an expansion project. Small asserts that this is not a taking for public use.

The trial testimony has concluded and closing arguments will occur after a short recess. Depending on what your professor decides, you may be an attorney for the City, an attorney for Small, or a judge. As an attorney, your job is to explain why your client should prevail in the case, considering both the law and the facts.

The arguments for both sides will focus on Justice Kennedy's concurrence in *Kelo*, which occupies a middle ground between the other four members of the majority and the four dissenters. Arguably, the Kennedy concurrence has become the *de facto* rule in public use cases. If Kennedy's test is not violated in a public use case, then he would presumably join with the *Kelo* majority in upholding a particular condemnation, as long as it served a public purpose. But if his test is violated, he would logically join with the *Kelo* dissenters in finding that the public use standard was not met; notice that under the approach taken by the *Kelo* dissenters, the condemnation in the exercise would not meet the public use standard because the land at issue does not cause any social harm.

The case file is below. It includes the complaint, the answer, and a partial transcript of the trial testimony. Both sides have access to the same facts in this exercise.

CITY HALL
47 MAIN STREET
TUSCULUM, MADISON 55442
(791) 550-2201

October 20, YR-02

Mr. Edward H. Small
8 Farm Estates Road
Tusculum, Madison 55442

Dear Mr. Small:

I represent the City in connection with the Tusculum Towers Casino improvement project. As you may know, the Casino will soon be adding a second hotel tower and a special casino facility designed to attract high-stakes gamblers. This project will benefit Tusculum and all of Seneca County by providing new employment opportunities, attracting more tourist dollars for local businesses, providing new recreational and housing options, and improving the economic climate in general.

In order for this project to proceed, it will be necessary for the Casino to obtain land for additional parking. The planned improvements are anticipated to increase the number of daytime and overnight patrons and will require 447 new parking spaces. Because approximately 150 parking spaces can be located on one acre of land, the Casino needs three acres of land for these parking facilities. The most suitable land for this use is a three acre parcel at the south end of your farm, which abuts the north side of the current Casino property. This is because the land immediately west of the current Casino property is a wetland and thus protected from development under Section 404 of the Clean Water Act, while the land east of the Casino property is too steep and rugged. This leaves your land, which is quite flat and not a protected wetland.

While the City regrets the necessity of acquiring your land, we hope that you will realize that all citizens must sometimes set aside their personal preferences in order to serve the common good. Of course, you will be fully compensated for the land. The county tax assessor has determined that the land has a fair market value of $60,000, and the City will soon be in a position to pay you this amount. We would prefer to make this a voluntary sale, rather than to use the power of eminent domain. Please have your attorney contact me to discuss this matter.

Sincerely,

Joseph F. Trezza

Joseph F. Trezza
City Attorney

LUTHER, STRAUSS & FROST
83 FIRST STREET, THIRD FLOOR
TUSCULUM, MADISON 55442-0558
791.550.2974
WWW.LUTHERFIRM.COM

November 15, YR-02

Joseph F. Trezza, Esq.
City of Tusculum
City Hall
47 Main Street
Tusculum, Madison 55442

Dear Mr. Trezza:

Our long-time client Edward Small has informed me that the city seeks to purchase part of his farm in order to provide additional parking for the new facilities which will be built at the Tusculum Towers Casino. Please be advised that Mr. Small is unwilling to sell his land at any price. Frankly, I am surprised that the city wants to take land from Mr. Small in order to give it to the casino. You will remember that a majority of Tusculum citizens opposed the original casino project when it was proposed—which is why the city council members who approved the project were voted out at the next election. It seems to me that the current city council is running exactly the same risk.

Although the three acres at issue constitute less than one percent of the Small farm, they have sentimental value to Mr. Small because the family has used part of this area as a pet cemetery for decades. Pets formerly owned by his parents and many of his relatives are buried there. Under these circumstances, it seems disrespectful that the city would seek to convert the land to a parking lot for gamblers.

The city does not have the power to take Mr. Small's land by eminent domain because the public use requirement cannot be met. The sole purpose of such an action would be to benefit one particular private party, the Tusculum Towers Casino Corporation, which I suspect asked the city to acquire the property in the first place. Moreover, the corporation could provide enough parking for the new facility simply by building a parking garage on the land which it now owns. Under these circumstances, any claim that the public would benefit from the condemnation of Mr. Small's land is implausible.

Very truly yours,

James P. Frost

James P. Frost

Fulton & Knight, LLP
102 Main Street
Tusculum, Madison 55442
(791) 550-8947

March 31, YR-01

James P. Frost, Esq.
Luther, Strauss & Frost
83 First Street, Third Floor
Tusculum, Madison 55442

Dear Mr. Frost:

I am representing the city in connection with its planned acquisition of certain land owned by your client Edward Small. Joe Trezza has provided me with your November 15 letter in this matter.

The city would very much prefer to handle this situation without litigation. Toward that end and solely to avoid the expense and delay of litigation, the city has authorized me to offer Mr. Small the sum of $110,000 for the three acres in question, which is more than twice what the land is worth. As you probably know, prime farm land around Tusculum is selling for between $18,000 and $20,000 per acre. Please tell me within two weeks whether your client is willing to accept this offer.

Turning to the balance of your letter, the city completely rejects your assertion that a condemnation of the land would not be a taking for public use. As the Supreme Court made clear in *Kelo v. City of New London*, the condemnation of property for the purpose of economic redevelopment is a public use. The project involved in *Kelo* included the construction of a hotel and new parking facilities, much like the casino project here. The economic analysis prepared by the city's outside consultant, Hargreaves & Associates, concludes that the casino project will create many new jobs and bring hundreds of thousands of dollars of tourist revenue to the region, in addition to providing other benefits to the public. I enclose a summary of this analysis for your review. Under these circumstances, the planned taking undeniably qualifies as a public use, whether the Tusculum Towers Casino Corporation requested it or not. Finally, your assertion that the corporation could build a parking garage on its own land is simply wrong because such a garage would cost so much that the entire project would not be economically viable.

Very truly yours,

Maria B. Fulton
Maria B. Fulton

Hargreaves & Associates

Economic Analysis & Planning
101 North Fifth Street, Suite 8C
Capital City, Madison 55492
790.313.7641
www.HargreavesAnalysis.net

ANALYSIS OF TUSCULUM TOWERS CASINO IMPROVEMENT PROJECT

EXECUTIVE SUMMARY

The Tusculum Towers Casino Improvement Project ("Project") will provide significant benefits to the City of Tusculum and Seneca County as a whole.

Employment: Currently, 7% of Tusculum residents are unemployed. It is projected that the Project will create 120 new jobs, which will lessen this problem. These positions will include dealers, restaurant servers, maids, and parking lot attendants. While most of these positions will be filled by workers who will be recruited from outside of Madison, it is possible that some of the new jobs may be filled by Seneca County residents who are currently unemployed.

Tourist revenue: The Project will create new facilities which could accommodate more than 600 additional customers per day. Assuming that the national economy improves to the point where there is sustained demand for such facilities, the Project could generate additional revenues of between $8 and $12 million per year. Although the existing casino complex successfully captures almost all of the revenues which customers spend in the region, it is possible that the Project would generate a total of between $10,000 and $20,000 per year in additional revenues for off-site local businesses.

Recreation: The Project will benefit local residents by providing greater opportunities for them to participate in recreational gambling, with a focus on high-stakes gambling.

Housing: The Project will benefit local residents by providing additional hotel rooms which can be used by their family members and friends who need a place to stay during visits.

Tax revenues: The Project will increase revenues for Tusculum from property taxes and gambling taxes. The amount is as yet undetermined, because the Madison Legislature is currently discussing bills which would transfer most of such taxes from cities and counties to the state.

This is only a summary of the Analysis and, by definition, should not be relied upon as definitive.
Persons interested in obtaining a complete copy of the Analysis should
contact Raymond Hargreaves at the above address.

MARIA B. FULTON
FULTON & KNIGHT, LLP
102 Main Street
Tusculum, Madison 55442
(791) 550-8947

Attorneys for Plaintiff

SUPERIOR COURT OF MADISON

COUNTY OF SENECA

CITY OF TUSCULUM,

        Plaintiff,   NO. 14-085

vs.

EDWARD H. SMALL,   COMPLAINT

        Defendant.

Plaintiff alleges as follows:

1. Plaintiff CITY OF TUSCULUM ("CITY") is a municipal corporation organized and existing under the laws of Madison and is by law vested with authority to exercise the power of eminent domain to acquire private property for public use.

2. CITY seeks to acquire by eminent domain fee simple absolute title to the following described real property ("Property") located in Seneca County, Madison:

> The southernmost 209 feet of Parcel 4 as shown on that certain subdivision map
> entitled "Tusculum Farm Estates," recorded in Book 22, Page 171, Seneca County
> Records, on October 3, 1922.

A map of the Property and the area surrounding it is attached hereto as Exhibit A.

3. Defendant EDWARD H. SMALL ("SMALL") is the owner of fee simple absolute title in the Property.

4. On February 8, YR-01, by a majority vote of its members and after due notice and opportunity to be heard, the CITY Council adopted a resolution of necessity ("Resolution") authorizing CITY to acquire the Property by eminent domain. A true and correct copy of the

Resolution is attached hereto as Exhibit B and incorporated fully by reference herein. As established by the Resolution: (a) the Tusculum Towers Casino improvement project will serve the public interest; (b) it is necessary for the CITY to acquire the Property from SMALL as part of the project; (c) the condemnation of the Property is for a public use; and (d) SMALL has refused the offer of compensation for the Property which was made pursuant to Madison Government Code § 897.17. The Resolution authorizes the CITY to acquire fee simple absolute title to the Property.

WHEREFORE, CITY prays for judgment as follows:

1. That the Property be condemned to CITY's use in fee simple absolute.

2. That just compensation be ascertained, assessed, and awarded as provided by law;

3. That all liens and encumbrances against the Property be deducted from the judgment; and

4. For such other and further relief as the Court may deem proper.

Dated: May 1, YR-01   FULTON & KNIGHT

                                        By: *Maria B. Fulton*
                                        MARIA B. FULTON

Map of Subject Property
Southernmost 209 feet of Parcel 4

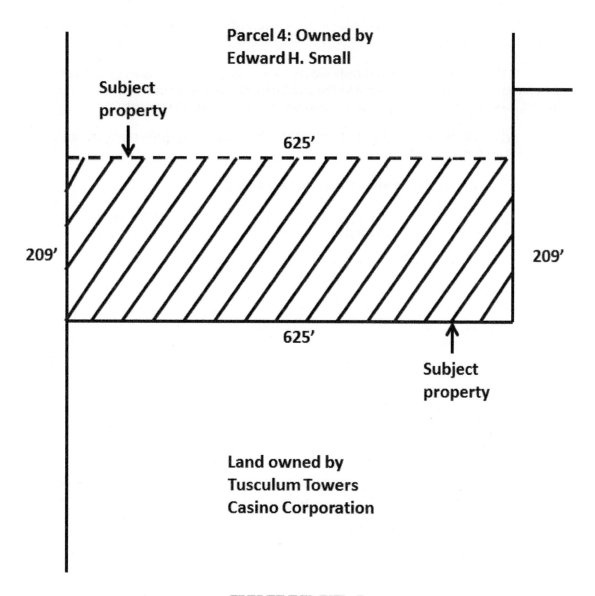

EXHIBIT A

CITY OF TUSCULUM

RESOLUTION OF NECESSITY TO CONDEMN REAL PROPERTY

WHEREAS Madison Government Code § 889.5 authorizes a city to acquire real property for economic redevelopment by eminent domain; and

WHEREAS the real property described herein is needed for the Tusculum Towers Casino improvement project; and

WHEREAS the City Council finds and determines that notice of its intention to adopt this Resolution was duly given as required by law and, on the date and at the time and place fixed for hearing, that the City Council did hear and consider all of the evidence presented;

NOW, THEREFORE, LET IT BE RESOLVED pursuant to Madison Government Code § 892 that the City Council hereby finds the following:

1.   The said project will serve the public interest.

2.   The real property sought to be acquired is necessary for the project and the condemnation is a taking for public use.

3.   The real property owner has refused the offer of compensation which was made pursuant to Madison Government Code § 897.17.

AND BE IT FURTHER RESOLVED that Maria B. Fulton, attorney with the firm of Fulton & Knight, as counsel for the City of Tusculum, is hereby authorized and directed to commence and maintain a proceeding in the Superior Court of the State of Madison, in and for the County of Seneca, to acquire for the City the fee simple absolute title in that certain real property which is described as follows:

The southernmost 209 feet of Parcel 4 as shown on the subdivision map entitled "Tusculum Farm Estates," recorded in Book 22, Page 171, Seneca County Records, on October 3, 1922.

THE FOREGOING WAS PASSED AND ADOPTED by the vote of the City Council this 8th day of February, YR-01.

AYES: Colella, Irvin, Morse, Weule
NOES: Santiago
ABSENT: None

Dianna Abbott
ATTEST: Diana Abbot, Clerk, City Council

EXHIBIT B

JAMES P. FROST
LUTHER, STRAUSS & FROST
83 First Street, Third Floor
Tusculum, Madison 55442
791.550.2974

Attorneys for Defendant

SUPERIOR COURT OF MADISON

COUNTY OF SENECA

CITY OF TUSCULUM,

         Plaintiff,   No. 14-085

vs.

EDWARD H. SMALL,   ANSWER

         Defendant.

Defendant EDWARD H. SMALL answers the Complaint as follows:

1. Defendant admits the allegations set forth in Paragraphs 1, 2, and 3.

2. Defendant admits the allegations set forth in Paragraph 4 that the City Council adopted a resolution of necessity on February 8, YR-01, by majority vote and after due notice and opportunity to be heard, that Exhibit B is a true and correct copy of that resolution, and that defendant refused an offer of compensation for the Property which the City made. Except as expressly admitted above, defendant denies each and every remaining allegation set forth in said paragraph.

WHEREFORE, defendant prays for judgment as follows:

1. That plaintiff take nothing by its Complaint herein;

2. For costs of suit incurred herein; and

3. For such other and further relief as the Court may deem proper.

Dated: May 25, YR-01   LUTHER, STRAUSS & FROST

                              By: *James P. Frost*
                              JAMES P. FROST

SUPERIOR COURT OF MADISON
COUNTY OF SENECA
3

4   CITY OF TUSCULUM,
5   Plaintiff,
6   vs.   No. 14-085
7   EDWARD H. SMALL,
8   Defendant.
9

10   EXCERPTS FROM TRIAL TRANSCRIPT
11   JANUARY 4, YR-00
12   BEFORE THE HONORABLE LISA Y. CHOU
13   For the plaintiff: MARIA B. FULTON, FULTON & KNIGHT
14   For defendant: JAMES P. FROST, LUTHER, STRAUSS & FROST
15   *   *   *   *   *
16   THE COURT: For the record, counsel for both sides have stipulated that Exhibits A and
17   B to the complaint in this action, the map and the resolution of necessity, may be admitted into
18   evidence and they are so admitted. Ms. Fulton, are you ready to proceed?
19   FULTON: Yes, your honor. We call Samuel Weule.
20   SAMUEL M. WEULE
21   called as a witness by the plaintiff, being first duly sworn, was examined and testified as follows:
22   DIRECT EXAMINATION
23   FULTON: Please state your full name and occupation for the record.
24   A. Samuel M. Weule. That's pronounced Wee-uh-lee. I'm the mayor of Tusculum.
25   Q. I show you Exhibit B, the resolution of necessity. Are you familiar with this
26   document?
27   A. Yes. And I voted for it, because it would benefit the city—the condemnation, I mean.
28   That would benefit everyone.
29   Q. Why would the condemnation of Mr. Small's land be beneficial?
30   A. For several reasons. Now I am not a financial expert by any means. But I have seen
31   the Hargreaves analysis which makes it clear that this project will create over 120 new jobs—

1   FROST: Objection your honor. This is hearsay.

2   THE COURT: Mr. Weule, you can only testify to your personal knowledge.

3   FULTON: Well, sir, at the time you voted for this condemnation, did you believe that it

4   would affect the employment rate in the Tusculum region?

5   A. I sure did. At that time we were running a 7% unemployment rate, which was a bit

6   lower than the state average, but higher than what we have seen in the past, which was about 5%.

7   I believed that the casino expansion project would create new jobs, about 120 new jobs—

8   FROST: Objection your honor. This is hearsay again.

9   FULTON: No, your honor. This goes to the witness's state of mind, his motivation.

10   THE COURT: Overruled. You may answer.

11   WITNESS: What was the question again?

12   FULTON: You were saying that the project would create 120 new jobs.

13   A. Right. And we needed those new jobs in our city. People were losing their homes in

14   foreclosure because they had no work.

15   Q. Were there any other benefits you thought the project would provide to the public?

16   A. Yes. We thought it would attract more tourists, who would spend money at all the

17   businesses in the area—restaurants, shops, and so on. Also, having more hotel rooms in the area

18   makes it easier for out-of-town visitors to visit people living here in Tusculum, because they

19   would have a place to stay. It's also a kind of recreation, gambling. People like to do it. Lots of

20   people from town go to the casino now for fun, and the expansion would give them even more

21   opportunity. And the project also would produce more tax revenue for the city.

22   Q. How much more tax revenue?

23   A. We don't know yet. Probably some, according to the Hargreaves analysis.

24   Q. How does Mr. Small's land relate to the project?

25   A. As I understand it, the project cannot be built without the Small land, because it's

26   needed for parking. If people can't park, they won't come.

27   Q. Does the city have a long-term plan about how it will grow in the future?

28   A. Yes, we are required to have one by state law.

29   Q. And does that plan say anything about economic development?

30   A. Yes. It's in Section 24.3.8. I've got it right here. It says: "City shall seek to improve

31   the local economy by encouraging business growth and expansion."

1   Q. Does the city have any other plan that deals with economic development?

2   A. No.

3   FULTON: That's all for now, your honor.

4   THE COURT: Any cross-examination?

5   <u>CROSS-EXAMINATION</u>

6   FROST: Mr. Weule, isn't it true that the idea for acquiring my client's land came from

7 the casino corporation, not from the city?

8   A. I'm not really sure. I guess it was a mutual thing. The casino folks . . . mainly Lillian

9 Keeling . . . were talking about expanding and the question of more parking naturally came up.

10   Q. Ms. Keeling is the casino complex manager, a vice president of the corporation which

11 owns it, the Tusculum Towers Casino Corporation?

12   A. Yes.

13   Q. And Ms. Keeling came up with the idea of taking my client's land?

14   FULTON: Objection. Asked and answered.

15   THE COURT: Overruled.

16   A. Like I just said, it was a mutual decision. Lillian mentioned the idea first, sure, but I

17 wanted the benefits of the project for the city, for all the citizens. And so did the rest of the

18 council, or most of them. To make that happen, there had to be more parking. Look, there are

19 only three properties which are next to the casino. One of them, to the west, is wetlands; you

20 can't pave that. On the other side, the east, you have rocky cliffs and so forth. So the Small land

21 was the only other possibility, on the north side. It is flat and buildable.

22   Q. Isn't it true that the casino corporation could have built a parking garage on the land it

23 already owned?

24   A. No, because that kind of garage would just be too expensive. It would make the whole

25 project financially impossible—

26   Q. Now, Mr. Weule, I'm only asking you to testify to what you know, not what someone

27 may have told you.

28   FULTON: Your honor, Mr. Frost opened the door. The witness is entitled to complete

29 his answer without being interrupted.

30   THE COURT: Mr. Weule, please finish your statement.

1   A. Like I was saying, a parking garage would be too expensive. It costs about $20,000

2   per space. That would be about $9,000,000 to build a parking garage. If the casino had to build

3   one, it would kill the project. Paving flat land is much, much cheaper, maybe $200 per space.

4   Q. Isn't it true that most of the jobs the project would create, about 80%, would be filled

5   by people who would be recruited from out of state?

6   A. I don't know the precise figure. Yes, some would come from out of state.

7   Q. So isn't it fair to say that any local employment benefits would be minor?

8   A. It depends on what you mean by minor. Even if 80% were from another state, 20%

9   would still be local, say 24 jobs.

10   Q. Let's move on. Now Exhibit B, the resolution of necessity, refers to something called

11   the "Tusculum Towers Casino improvement project." Is it correct that only two parcels of land

12   will be directly affected by that project: the casino parcel and my client's land?

13   A. Yes.

14   Q. Then, just so we're clear, this is a case about two owners: the corporation which is

15   benefited by the condemnation, and my client who is harmed, right?

16   A. Not really. I think everyone in the city would benefit.

17   Q. Isn't it true that the Tusculum Towers Casino Corporation contributed $10,000 to your

18   campaign for mayor two years ago? It was your biggest single donation by far.

19   A. Look, my vote can't be bought, if that's what you're suggesting. Sure, it is true that

20   the casino was my biggest single donor, but then the casino is the biggest business in town. They

21   contributed to my campaign because they shared my view that Tusculum needed to grow, to

22   develop, to create new jobs. And remember that this whole expansion thing surfaced long ago,

23   before I even thought about running for mayor.

24   Q. You made it clear to the other members of the council during the public hearing that

25   you strongly supported the condemnation plan, right?

26   A. Yes, I suppose so. That was my position.

27   Q. And if some of the council members were undecided on the issue, your strong support

28   for the plan would have led them to support it as well, isn't that correct?

29   FULTON: Objection. Calls for speculation.

30   FROST: Your honor, I'll withdraw the question. I have nothing further for this witness.

31   THE COURT: Ms. Fulton, please call your next witness.

1   FULTON: Your honor, I call Lillian Keeling.
2   LILLIAN BETHANY KEELING
3   called as a witness by plaintiff, being first duly sworn, was examined and testified as follows:
4   DIRECT EXAMINATION
5   FULTON: State your name and occupation for the record, please.
6   A. Lillian Bethany Keeling. I'm a vice president of the Tusculum Towers Casino
7   Corporation.
8   Q. Ms. Keeling, are you familiar with the planned expansion of the casino?
9   A. Yes.
10   Q. Would it be possible to implement that project without acquiring Mr. Small's land?
11   A. No.
12   Q. Why not?
13   A. The economy is weak right now, so the project is marginal to start with. We're taking
14   a big risk that things will get better. If we had to build a parking garage on site, it would cost
15   about $9,000,000, as the mayor just said. That extra expense would kill the project. The
16   economics could not justify it. So the expansion is only possible with surface parking. That
17   means we would have to acquire part of the Small land for parking.
18   Q. Ms. Keeling, the attorney for Mr. Small seems to be implying that there was some sort
19   of conspiracy between the casino and the city. Is there any truth to that claim?
20   A. None whatsoever. It just so happens that our interests are aligned. The expansion will
21   bring more jobs to Tusculum, more tourist revenue, and so forth. Yes, the casino will benefit.
22   But the citizens of Tusculum will also benefit.
23   FULTON: Your honor, I have no more questions at this time.
24   THE COURT: Cross-examination, counsel?
25   CROSS-EXAMINATION
26   FROST: Yes, your honor. Isn't it true that about 80% of the new jobs would be filled by
27   people that your company recruits from outside of Madison?
28   A. I'm not sure about the percentage. It would probably be a majority of the new jobs,
29   maybe 80%.
30   Q. Well, using the 80% figure, this would mean that only 24 new jobs would be created
31   for local residents, right?

1   A. Yes, if that estimate is correct.

2   Q. And isn't it true that most of these jobs would pay only the minimum wage?

3   A. That's true for the maids and parking lot attendants, but not the dealers. And the

4 servers would get tips.

5   Q. But isn't it true that the new jobs for local residents would be for maids and parking

6 lot attendants?

7   A. I can't say that for sure. But yes, we would probably hire some locals for jobs like

8 that.

9   Q. Let's turn to another issue. Is it fair to say that your company's goal is to ensure that

10 casino patrons spend their money at shops and restaurants inside the casino complex, rather than

11 spending that money outside the complex?

12   A. Yes, I think that's right. We try to be a full service resort.

13   Q. Then isn't it true that the additional patrons resulting from the expansion project

14 would also spend their money inside the casino complex, not in local shops and businesses?

15   A. Well, it's not like we keep our customers in a prison. Even now, they occasionally

16 eat in local restaurants off the casino property and shop in local souvenir shops.

17   Q. But doesn't your company view this as a failure which you would like to correct?

18   A. I suppose so. We would like our customers to spend their money with us.

19   Q. Isn't it true that your corporation came up with the idea of taking Mr. Small's land, not

20 the city?

21   A. As I recall, it was the product of a discussion between people from the city and people

22 from the casino about how to proceed, given the difficulties with parking. Maybe I said it first, I

23 don't know.

24   Q. Now you are aware that your company gave $10,000 to Mr. Weule's campaign for

25 mayor, right?

26   A. Yes.

27   Q. And you were involved in the decision to make that donation, weren't you?

28   A. I was consulted, yes.

29   Q. You recommended that such a donation be made, right?

30   A. Yes, I thought it was a good idea.

1   Q. And you thought it was a good idea because a mayor who was on your side would

2   help to get the expansion project approved, right?

3   A. I thought that Mr. Weule wanted Tusculum to grow and its businesses to flourish . . .

4   that he would be "pro-business" as a general matter, not that there would be some sort of secret

5   deal. Anyway, the resolution of necessity would have passed even without his vote.

6   FROST: I have nothing further.

7   *   *   *   *   *

8   THE COURT: Ms. Fulton, do you wish to call any additional witnesses?

9   FULTON: No, your honor. The plaintiff rests.

10   THE COURT: Mr. Frost, you may call your first witness.

11   FROST: Your honor, I call Edward Small.

12   EDWARD H. SMALL

13   called as a witness by defendant, being first duly sworn, was examined and testified as follows:

14   DIRECT EXAMINATION

15   FROST: Ed, please state your name and occupation for the record.

16   A. Edward H. Small. I'm a farmer.

17   Q. Now you're the owner of about 420 acres of farm land in Tusculum, including the

18   three acres at issue in this case, right?

19   A. Yes, that's right.

20   Q. What estate do you have in that three acre parcel?

21   A. As I understand it, I have a fee simple absolute estate.

22   Q. And what do you use the land for?

23   A. Most years I grow corn on part of it. Sometimes soybeans.

24   Q. Do the three acres at issue have any special significance to you?

25   FULTON: Objection, your honor. It's irrelevant.

26   FROST: Your honor—

27   THE COURT: I'll allow it. Proceed.

28   A. Well, my family has been burying our dead pets there for many years, for

29   decades—dogs, cats, a pet sheep, and some goats. Not on all of it, of course, but a big chunk of

30   maybe an acre. There is a small headstone with the name of each pet. I don't farm that spot. To

31   me, it's a special place.

1   Q. Did you ever have a phone conversation with Mr. Weule about why he supported the

2 idea of condemning your land?

3   A. Yes, I did. It was in February, just before there was a vote on the resolution.

4   Q. And what did he say during that call about the condemnation?

5   A. He said that the casino was important to him and to Tusculum, or something like that.

6   Q. Can you be more specific?

7   A. It was something about him retiring soon, and then he would be taken care of. That he

8 wouldn't have to worry.

9   FROST: Nothing further, your honor.

10   THE COURT: Ms. Fulton, do you want to cross-examine?

11   CROSS-EXAMINATION

12   FULTON: Yes, your honor. Mr. Small, are you testifying here today that Mr. Weule

13 told you that the casino had bribed him or was going to bribe him? Is that your testimony?

14   A. I didn't say that. And no, he didn't say that. Not exactly.

15   *   *   *   *

16   FULTON: Your honor, I would like to recall Mr. Weule at this time.

17   THE COURT: Mr. Weule, would you please come forward? Remember that you are

18 still under oath.

19   SAMUEL M. WEULE

20   DIRECT EXAMINATION

21   FULTON: Mr. Weule, did you hear Mr. Small testify earlier today about a telephone

22 conversation that you allegedly had with him last February?

23   A. Yes, I did.

24   Q. During that call, or at any other time, did you tell Mr. Small that the casino had bribed

25 you?

26   A. No, absolutely not.

27   Q. Or was going to bribe you?

28   A. No.

29   Q. Or words to that effect?

30   A. No.

1   Q. Did you say anything at all during that call about being taken "care of" or not having
2   to "worry"?
3   A. I might have said something along the lines that any extra taxes from the casino
4   expansion could improve the city's financial position, so that none of the city's retired
5   employees would have to worry about whether the city could afford to keep paying for their
6   health insurance. And I guess that would include me, since I was planning not to run for
7   reelection.
8   FULTON: Nothing further, your honor.
9   *   *   *   *   *
10   THE COURT: As I understand it, both sides have now rested. Is that correct?
11   FULTON: Yes, your honor.
12   FROST: Yes, your honor.
13   THE COURT: Then we'll take a fifteen minute break. When we reconvene, we'll have
14   closing arguments.

Chapter 12

Takings

A. INTRODUCTION

The exercise in this chapter involves the law of takings—perhaps the most challenging topic in property law today. The Takings Clause of the Fifth Amendment mandates compensation when private property is "taken" for public use. But it is often difficult to determine when a "taking" occurs.

This is a negotiation exercise based on a dispute between a landowner and the federal government. The owner claims that the use of his land by the U.S. Drug Enforcement Administration constitutes a taking for which compensation must be paid, while the federal government denies this. You will act as an attorney either for the owner or the government in trying to resolve the dispute, using Supreme Court decisions that have interpreted the Takings Clause.

The first section of this chapter is a basic introduction to the complex law of takings. The next section provides you with two new techniques to use in the negotiation. The final section is the case file of documents relevant to the dispute.

B. OVERVIEW OF THE LAW

1. FOUR TESTS

The modern law of takings is defined by a series of Supreme Court decisions. The general standard to determine whether a taking has occurred is a multi-factor balancing test first set forth in *Penn Central Transportation Co. v. City of New York*, 438 U.S. 104 (1978), which is discussed below. In later years, the Court developed three specialized or "categorical" tests to supplement the *Penn Central* standard. Under these tests, a taking will be found where a government entity:

(a) authorizes a permanent physical occupation of land—*Loretto v. Teleprompter Manhattan CATV Corp.*, 458 U.S. 419 (1982);

(b) adopts a regulation that causes the loss of all economically beneficial or productive use of land, unless justified by background principles of property or nuisance law—*Lucas v. South Carolina Coastal Council*, 505 U.S. 1003 (1992); or

(c) demands an exaction, in exchange for a discretionary land use approval, that has no essential nexus to a legitimate state interest or lacks rough proportionality to the impacts of the project—*Nollan v. California*

Coastal Commission, 483 U.S. 825 (1987) and *Dolan v. City of Tigard*, 512 U.S. 374 (1994).

The two key decisions potentially relevant to the exercise are *Loretto* and *Penn Central*, which are discussed in more detail below.

2. SPECIALIZED TEST FROM *LORETTO*

Loretto arose from a complex fact situation. In 1970, the owner of a New York apartment building allowed the local cable television company to install a cable and related equipment on the building roof, in return for 5% of the gross revenues that the company received from the property. The cable was about 34–36 feet long and less than ½ inch in diameter; it was attached to the roof masonry with screws or nails. The cable company also attached two directional taps (each a 4 inch cube) and two large silver boxes to the roof with bolts. These facilities did not initially serve the building, but rather were part of a system that served other buildings on the block. Loretto purchased the apartment building one year later. Effective January 1, 1973, a new state statute provided that a landlord could not interfere with the installation of cable television facilities on his property, and would receive a one-time payment of $1.00 as compensation for the use of the property; this effectively nullified the revenue-sharing agreement. Subsequently, the cable company installed a line down the front of Loretto's building, which provided service to her tenants. Loretto brought a class action, asserting that these installations constituted a taking without just compensation.

In *Loretto*, the Supreme Court affirmed what it called the "historical rule" that "a permanent physical occupation of another's property is a taking" even if it is minor in scope. 458 U.S. at 435. It reasoned that such an occupation effectively destroys the owner's rights to possess, use, and dispose of her property. In a footnote, the Court distinguished between a *permanent physical occupation* and a *temporary invasion*. It stressed that "[n]ot every physical *invasion* is a taking," noting that "such temporary limitations are subject to a more complex balancing process. . ." *Id.* The rationale for this distinction, it explained, was that temporary invasions "do not absolutely dispossess the owner of his rights to use, and exclude others from, his property." *Id.* Accordingly, even if government conduct is not a permanent physical occupation, but rather a temporary invasion, it still might be a taking under the *Penn Central* test.

3. GENERAL TEST FROM *PENN CENTRAL*

The *Penn Central* case involved the application of New York City's Landmarks Preservation Law to Grand Central Terminal. The owner of the terminal leased the valuable air space above the terminal, so that an office building could be constructed there. Because the terminal was classified as a landmark, approval from a city commission was required for any new construction on the site. After the commission refused permission for two project proposals (a 53-story building and a 55-story building), the owner and the lessee sued on a takings theory.

In *Penn Central*, the Court used a new, three-factor balancing test in deciding that no taking had occurred. The factors it considered were: (a) the economic impact of the regulation on the claimant; (b) the extent to which the regulation has interfered with distinct investment-backed expectations; and (c) the character of the government action.

a. Economic impact: This factor considers the extent of the economic loss suffered by the owner as a result of the government action, usually measured by diminution in market value. The *Penn Central* court noted that the plaintiffs had not shown any loss, because nothing the commission had done suggested it would prohibit all construction above the terminal; thus, a smaller building might well be permitted. The Court also emphasized that the terminal owner could receive compensation for its development rights by transferring them to another parcel.

b. Investment-backed expectations: This factor focuses on the owner's reasonable expectations at the time she purchased the property. The Court observed that the commission's decisions did not prevent the owner from operating the terminal as it had for the prior 65 years, which was its "primary expectation concerning the use of the parcel." 438 U.S. at 136.

c. Character of the government action: The decision states that a taking will more readily be found when the interference stems from a physical invasion by government, rather than by a government program—such as a regulation—adjusting the benefits and burdens of economic life to promote the common good. Here, the government action did not involve any physical invasion, but rather was a reasonable regulation designed to promote the general welfare.

Today the balancing test used in *Penn Central* is the *general test* that is used to determine if a taking exists, if no taking is found under any of the potentially applicable *specialized tests* discussed above.

4. DAMAGES

If a taking is found, the normal remedy is that the property owner receives compensatory damages. The requirement of "just compensation" in the Takings Clause is usually equated with *fair market value*: the price that a willing seller would accept and a willing buyer would pay for a particular property on the open market. In the case of a temporary taking, the measure of damages is the *fair rental value* of the property during the period while it was taken: the price that a willing landlord would accept and a willing tenant would pay to rent a particular property on the open market.

C. NEGOTIATION TECHNIQUES

Remember the techniques you learned in earlier chapters:

1. *Develop a plan for the negotiation.*

2. *Set appropriate goals for the negotiation.*

3. *Envision the negotiation from the other side's perspective.*

4. *Develop two goals: an aspirational goal and a bottom-line goal.*

5. *Ask questions.*

6. *Revisit the plan.*

7. *Keep in mind your BATNA.*

8. *Be willing to walk away.*

9. *Negotiate from interests, not positions.*

10. *Use legitimizing sources.*

11. *Search for mutual benefit.*

12. *Watch body language.*

This section will introduce you to two additional techniques:

13. *Be reluctant to split the difference.* It is normal for both sides to make concessions during the course of a negotiation. At some point, the parties may be so close together in a monetary negotiation that one side may ask the other side to "split the difference" between their offers. This is often done by an inexperienced negotiator who is more interested in finding a quick method of ending the negotiation than in best protecting the interests of her client. Most of the time, the proper response to a split-the-difference offer is to treat it as a concession and make a counter-offer. That said, it may be appropriate to split the difference if it is clear that no better deal is possible.

14. *Do not show triumph.* Even if you are extremely pleased by the result of the negotiation, be careful not to show this to the other side. If one negotiator displays triumph or similar pleasure at the outcome, the other side will realize that it could have made a better deal, and this creates the risk that the deal will unravel. The result of any negotiation is more likely to hold if each side believes that it has made a good deal.

D. THE IRWIN CLAIM

In this exercise, Anthony F. Irwin owns a large tract of desert land, which includes a dry lake bed. The U.S. Drug Enforcement Administration has been secretly using part of this land as an occasional landing site for its planes in connection with its efforts to search out drug smugglers from Mexico, without paying compensation to Irwin. Irwin argues that the DEA action constitutes a taking for which he should be compensated. The U.S. Department of Justice, representing the federal government, denies that any taking occurred. Assuming that a taking did occur, the two sides have quite different ideas about the amount of compensation which would be appropriate. You will be an attorney either for Irwin or the Justice Department in a negotiation to resolve the dispute.

Read the case file below to begin preparing for the negotiation. In addition to the file, your professor will give you confidential information concerning your side of the negotiation. As you work on your negotiation plan, be sure to consider: (1) Is the government action a *permanent physi-*

cal occupation under the *Loretto* test?; (2) Is the government action a *temporary invasion* that constitutes a taking under the *Penn Central* test?; and (3) If a taking has occurred, what is the appropriate amount of damages?

Laskin & Sawada
78 Central Avenue, Suite 420
Orinda, Madison 55428
(790) 378-0998

November 14, YR-01

Ms. Sheila Ward
Deputy Administrator of Operations
U.S. Drug Enforcement Agency
600 M Street, N.W., Suite 300
Washington, D.C. 20001

Dear Ms. Ward:

I represent Anthony F. Irwin, who is the owner of approximately 5,600 acres of land located in Madison, roughly 20 miles southeast of the town of Deep Spring. Mr. Irwin has recently learned that your agency has been occupying his land and utilizing it as an airport—without his approval. Mr. Irwin strongly objects to this taking of his private property.

Part of Mr. Irwin's property consists of a dry lake bed, about 1,300 acres in size, which is almost perfectly flat and thus is a suitable landing site for small planes. It appears that for some time your agency has been using perhaps 10% of the lake bed in connection with its efforts to search out drug smugglers across the border with Mexico. Based on Mr. Irwin's personal observations over some days, we know that, on average, a plane owned by your agency lands on the lake bed once every two weeks, usually remaining on the land overnight, until it flies off the next day. In addition, it seems that two or three employees of your agency sometimes live in tents located on the land; the tents are physically staked into the ground surface. Fuel, food, and other agency supplies are occasionally stored on the land as well.

Neither your agency nor any other part of the federal government—or any government—ever asked Mr. Irwin for permission to use his land. Nor did he ever provide such permission. Accordingly, the conduct of your agency as described above constitutes a taking of Mr. Irwin's private property for which he is entitled to just compensation under the Takings Clause of the Fifth Amendment.

It is not clear to Mr. Irwin how long your agency has been illegally using his property. Please provide this information to me within seven business days so that I can formulate a precise demand of the amount to which Mr. Irwin is entitled for the taking of his property.

Very truly yours,

Sandra C. Laskin

Sandra C. Laskin

UNITED STATES DEPARTMENT OF JUSTICE
950 PENNSYLVANIA AVENUE, NW
WASHINGTON, DC 20530-0001
(202) 514-2000

December 23, YR-01

Ms. Sandra C. Laskin
Laskin & Sawada
78 Central Avenue, Suite 420
Orinda, Madison 55428

Dear Ms. Laskin:

Sheila Ward, the Deputy Administrator of Operations for the U.S. Drug Enforcement Agency (DEA), has forwarded your recent letter to me for response. Please direct all future communications regarding this matter to me, not to Ms. Ward.

In response to your questions, the facts as I understand them are as follows. Airplanes owned or leased by the DEA have landed on a small portion of Mr. Irwin's property on approximately sixteen occasions during the last seven months. On three occasions, the DEA plane remained on the ground no longer than a matter of hours, leaving when a suspicious aircraft approached the region. On the other occasions, when no such aircraft appeared, the DEA airplane remained on the ground overnight, leaving the next day. These infrequent visits were part of the DEA effort to interdict clandestine efforts to smuggle drugs into the United States from Mexico. By definition, these limited operations had to be kept confidential from all members of the public, including Mr. Irwin. If the cartels had learned about the DEA presence in the Deep Spring region, our interdiction efforts would not have been as successful as they have proven to be. It appears that a few DEA employees did pitch a tent on the property on the occasions when an airplane remained there overnight. However, I am pleased to inform you that due to the success of its efforts in the region, it is likely that the DEA will be using the land only a few more times in the future.

I reject the claim that these actions constituted a taking of Mr. Irwin's property. You appear to be relying on *Loretto v. Teleprompter Manhattan CATV Corp.*, 458 U.S. 419 (1982), where the Supreme Court held that a "permanent physical occupation" would be a taking. However, even setting aside the important public purpose which was served by the limited DEA actions on Mr. Irwin's land, the *Loretto* standard was not met here. Assuming *arguendo* that the DEA presence was "physical," it was neither "permanent" nor an "occupation."

Very truly yours,

Jason Earl Saunders

Jason Earl Saunders
Senior Attorney

Laskin & Sawada

78 Central Avenue, Suite 420
Orinda, Madison 55428
(790) 378-0998

January 28, YR-00

Jason Earl Saunders, Esq.
Senior Attorney
U.S. Department of Justice
950 Pennsylvania Avenue, N.W.
Washington, D.C. 20530-0001

Dear Mr. Saunders:

Thank you for your December 23 letter. I appreciate the opportunity to clarify my client's position in this matter, which you seem to have misunderstood. As I indicated in my prior letter to you, the DEA's occupation of Mr. Irwin's land constitutes a taking in violation of the Fifth Amendment. We believe that, under the circumstances of this case, a strong argument can be made that this usage was indeed a permanent physical occupation under *Loretto*. In effect, the DEA was using Mr. Irwin's land as an airport, which is a type of permanent, physical use.

Alternatively, if this situation can somehow be viewed as a temporary invasion of the land, then it constitutes a taking under *Penn Central Transportation Co. v. City of New York*, 438 U.S. 104 (1978). First, the economic impact of the DEA occupation on Mr. Irwin is severe. As shown on the attached appraisal, the fair rental value of the property at issue is $455,000; to date, Mr. Irwin has been deprived of this sum. Second, while Mr. Irwin admittedly had no expectation that the DEA would secretly use his land as an airport at the time he purchased the land, he certainly did anticipate that he would be able to use it at any time for any purpose—an expectation which would have been frustrated by DEA agents had he even attempted to hike past their illegal encampment. Finally, as you are well aware, *Penn Central* provides that a taking is more likely to be found when "the interference with property can be characterized as a physical invasion by government" rather than as mere regulation.

Accordingly, I hereby demand that the federal government pay the sum of $455,000 to Mr. Irwin. If such payment is not made, we will have no choice but to bring suit.

Very truly yours,

Sandra C. Laskin

Sandra C. Laskin

Cassandri Real Estate Advisors
Appraisal • Consulting • Planning
530 North Third Street
Orinda, Madison 55428

January 22, YR-00

Sandra C. Laskin, Esq.
Laskin & Sawada
78 Central Avenue, Suite 420
Orinda, Madison 55428

Re: Appraisal of 130+/- Acres of Land Near Deep Spring, Madison

Dear Ms. Laskin:

I hereby submit my report assessing the fair rental value of certain land owned by your client Mr. Anthony F. Irwin, which is located southeast of Deep Spring, Madison.

This appraisal is based on the following assumptions: (a) the U.S. Drug Enforcement Agency (DEA) utilized approximately 10% of a 1,300 acre lake bed parcel owned by Mr. Irwin, or 130 acres, during the seven month period between approximately May and November of last year; (b) this use by the DEA precluded Mr. Irwin from utilizing the land; and (c) accordingly, the purpose of the report is to determine the fair rental value of the land during this period. After inspecting the land and analyzing the data as presented, I estimate that the fair rental value of the property during this period was: $455,000.

This valuation is based on a market analysis of the rental value of two sample properties discussed in detail in Appendix I which are reasonably proximate to the subject property, with appropriate adjustments: (a) <u>Weaver property</u>: 20 acres located within two miles of subject property, leased for cattle grazing for one year at the rate of $200 per acre per month; and (b) <u>Gizelle property</u>: 100 acres located within approximately 55 miles of subject property, leased for airport use at the rate of $600 per acre per month. Because the Gizelle property is improved for airport use with a runway and related facilities, its fair rental value is somewhat higher than the subject property. The Weaver property, which is geographically closer to the subject property, indicates that the normal value of land in the region without any improvements is $200 per acre per month. Combining the two figures, the reasonable rental value of the subject property is $500 per acre per month, or approximately $455,000 for seven months.

Respectfully submitted,

Joseph Cassandri
Joseph L. Cassandri

UNITED STATES DEPARTMENT OF JUSTICE
950 PENNSYLVANIA AVENUE, NW
WASHINGTON, DC 20530-0001
(202) 514-2000

February 17, YR-00

Ms. Sandra C. Laskin
Laskin & Sawada
78 Central Avenue, Suite 420
Orinda, Madison 55428

Re: Claim of Anthony F. Irwin

Dear Ms. Laskin:

Thank you for your recent letter concerning this matter.

Your contention that the DEA's rare, brief, and sporadic use of a small part of Mr. Irwin's land somehow constitutes a taking under *Loretto* has no basis in law or fact for the reasons set forth in my earlier letter.

Your new assertion that a taking has occurred under the *Penn Central* standard is similarly incorrect. First, as the enclosed appraisal by Eileen Miranda demonstrates, the economic impact on your client was *de minimis*: $38.17 at the most. Second, there is no indication that the investment-backed expectations of your client have been in any way frustrated. As to the third factor, it is important to consider the reason for the government's very limited use of this land: to protect all citizens, including Mr. Irwin, from the serious harms which arise from drug smuggling. These harms include criminal activity (such as homicides due to drug-related violence), permanent injuries to drug users, and harm to the national economy due to lack of productivity. This is, in short, a program designed to "promote the common good," which is insulated from liability under the *Penn Central* standard.

However, without admitting any liability, and solely in the interest of avoiding potentially costly litigation, I have been authorized to offer Mr. Irwin the sum of $100 in order to settle this matter. I should note that this amount is higher than the true rental value incurred to date because it is possible that DEA airplanes and employees may use the Irwin land on a few more occasions in the future. I look forward to your prompt response to this offer.

Very truly yours,

Jason Earl Saunders

Jason Earl Saunders
Senior Attorney

Eileen Miranda & Associates Appraisal Service
287 South First Street, Suite 830
Orinda, Madison 55428

February 12, YR-00

Jason E. Saunders, Esq.
Senior Attorney
U.S. Department of Justice
950 Pennsylvania Avenue, NW
Washington, D.C. 20530

Re: Appraisal of Irwin Land

Dear Mr. Saunders:

As you requested, I have (1) assessed the fair rental value of the portion of the 1,300 acres of land owned by Anthony F. Irwin which has been sporadically utilized by the U.S. Drug Enforcement Administration (DEA) and (2) analyzed the valuation letter relating to that property which was prepared by one Joseph Cassandri.

This valuation study is based on the following assumptions: (a) DEA airplanes and personnel used a portion of the Irwin land on sixteen occasions, on average for twelve hours each time (equal to 8 days in total, or about .266 months); and (b) on each occasion, the DEA used approximately 50,000 square feet of land, or 1.148 acres (based on 50 foot wingspan of airplane and need for 1,000 feet of land surface for takeoff). Based on these assumptions, my inspection of the property, and consideration of rental values for comparable properties, I conclude that the fair rental value of the land for the period it was used would be: $38.17.

The land in question is undeveloped, barren desert land consisting of a dry lake bed. There is no rental market for such land because it has no viable economic use. Within a radius of ten miles, there are sparsely-vegetated properties which are leased for cattle grazing. The average rental value of the 23 sample cattle grazing leases discussed in Appendix A is $125 per acre per month. The subject property has a lower rental value than these parcels because it contains no vegetation and is unsuitable for grazing. Still, assuming a fair rental value of $125 per acre per month, the 1.148 acres used for .266 months equates to $38.17 in rent.

The Cassandri valuation letter vastly overstates the relevant rental value because: (a) it assumes the DEA used 130 acres continuously for seven months; (b) it relies on the rental value of the Gizelle property which has a runway and other airport improvements, which is in no way comparable to the dry lake bed involved here; and (c) it examines only one grazing lease, without considering a sufficiently large sample of leases.

Sincerely,

Eileen Miranda
Eileen Miranda, MAI